The Millennial Investor: Simple Strategies for Long-Term Wealth

Daniel Hamlin

All rights reserved.

ISBN:

CONTENTS

Introduction

Section 1: The Basics

1. Understanding Your Finances: Getting a grip on income, expenses, and net worth.
2. Budgeting for Success: How to create and stick to a budget that works.
3. Emergency Funds and Financial Safety: Why they are crucial and how to build them.
4. Debt Management: Strategies for managing and reducing debt efficiently.
5. Savings Strategies: Best practices for saving systematically in your 20s and 30s.

Section 2: The Importance of Wealth Growth

6. The Power of Compounding: How your money grows over time.
7. Introduction to Investment Vehicles: Overview of bonds, stocks, mutual funds, and more.
8. Planning For Early Retirement: Understanding pensions, IRAs, and other retirement accounts.
9. Real Estate as an Investment: Basics of investing in property.
10. Alternative Investments: Exploring cryptocurrencies, commodities, and other non-traditional options.

Section 3: Investing in the Stock Market

11. Stock Market Basics: Understanding the market's structure and key concepts.
12. Types of Stocks: Differentiating between blue-chip, dividend, growth stocks, etc.
13. Fundamentals of Trading: An introduction to trading, including day trading vs. long-term investing.
14. Risk Management: How to assess and manage investment risk.
15. Building a Portfolio: Strategies for creating a diversified investment portfolio.

Section 4: Side Hustles

16. Identifying Profitable Side Hustles: How to find the right-side hustle for you.
17. E-commerce and Online Businesses: Setting up an online shop or service.
18. Freelancing: Leveraging your skills in the gig economy.
19. Real Estate and Passive Income: Tips for getting started with rental properties.
20. Turning Hobbies into Income: Case studies of successful personal enterprises.

Section 5: Investing in Yourself

21. The Winning Mentality: Developing the mindset for success.
22. Lifelong Learning: Importance of continuous education and where to focus.
23. Health and Wealth: How good health supports financial success.
24. Networking and Relationships: Building social capital for personal and professional growth.
25. Work-Life Balance: Maintaining balance for long-term happiness and productivity.

Conclusion
Helpful links
Glossary

Disclaimer for "The Millennial Investor: Simple Strategies for Long-Term Wealth"

This book, "The Millennial Investor: Simple Strategies for Long-Term Wealth," is intended solely for informational and educational purposes. The content provided herein does not constitute financial advice, investment advice, or any other type of advice, nor should it be treated as a substitute for professional advice, consultation or service. The information contained within this book is not tailored to the individual needs of any specific person, group or entity.

The author, Alex, and the publisher do not guarantee the accuracy, completeness, or usefulness of any information presented and are not responsible for any errors or omissions, or for results obtained from the use of this information. All information is provided "as is" without warranty of any kind.

While the strategies and information shared in this book are based on the author's personal experiences and the experiences of those he has advised, you should always conduct your own due diligence and consider your personal financial situation before acting on any of the topics discussed herein. It is strongly recommended that you seek advice from a qualified professional who is aware of your individual circumstances before making any financial decisions.

The author and publisher specifically disclaim any liability, loss or risk, personal or otherwise, which is incurred as a consequence, directly or indirectly, of the application and use of any of the contents of this book. By reading this book, you agree that the author and publisher of this book are not responsible for your personal actions in any way.

Introduction to "The Millennial Investor: Simple Strategies for Long-Term Wealth"

Welcome to "The Millennial Investor," your essential guide to navigating the complexities of personal finance and investment as a young adult in the 21st century. Whether you are fresh out of college, starting your first job, or already a few years into your career, this book is designed to help you lay a solid financial foundation and secure a prosperous future.

In these pages, Alex, a seasoned investor who started his journey much like you, shares his experiences and the valuable lessons learned along the way. Through a mix of personal anecdotes, straightforward advice, and actionable strategies, Alex will guide you through the essential steps to achieving financial independence and long-term wealth.

Why is this book different? Because it understands you. It speaks to the unique challenges and opportunities that millennials face in today's economic landscape—from navigating student loans and the gig economy to investing in cryptocurrencies and starting online businesses. "The Millennial Investor" is not just about investing money; it is about investing in yourself, your future, and transforming the way you interact with money.

You will learn how to:

- Craft a budget that allows you to enjoy life while saving for the future.
- Use the power of compound interest to your advantage.
- Diversify your investment portfolio to minimize risk and maximize returns!
- Harness the potential of real estate and stock markets!
- Build and leverage a professional network to open new opportunities!
- Balance achieving wealth with maintaining health and personal relationships.

By the end of this book, you will have a clearer understanding of where you stand financially and where you want to go. You will be equipped with the knowledge and tools to make informed decisions, invest wisely, and manage your money with confidence.

Join Alex on this journey of financial discovery and empowerment. It is time to turn your ambitions into achievements and reshape your financial future. Let us get started!

The Millennial Investor: Simple Strategies for Long-Term Wealth.

CHAPTER 1: UNDERSTANDING YOUR FINANCES

Welcome to the first step of your investing journey in "The Millennial Investor: Simple Strategies for Long-Term Wealth." I am Alex, and I will be your guide as we navigate the sometimes turbulent but always rewarding world of personal finance. Today, we start with a crucial foundation: understanding exactly where you stand financially. Whether you are just finishing school, starting your first job, or trying to untangle your finances, knowing your current position is essential.

Understanding Your Financial Status:
First, let us gather some basic information about your financial life. You will need to know your total income, how much you spend, what you own, and what you owe. It sounds simple, but many people, including myself in my early twenties, overlook this step. I once thought I had more money to invest than I actually did, which led me to make risky choices that weren't right for my situation. To avoid that, we will break this down into manageable parts.

Creating a Personal Balance Sheet:
A personal balance sheet will show your assets (what you own) and liabilities (what you owe). The difference between these is your net worth. Here is how to set it up:

List your assets: This includes your bank account balances, investments, and major personal items like your car or home.
List your liabilities: Include all debts such as student loans, credit card balances, and mortgages.
Calculate your net worth: Subtract your total liabilities from your total assets.
Analysing Income and Expenses:
Next, examine your income and expenses. One effective way to manage your finances is by using the 70:20:10 rule:

Seventy percent of your income should go towards essential expenses, such as rent, groceries, bills, and other necessities.

The Millennial Investor: Simple Strategies for Long-Term Wealth.

Twenty percent of your income should be allocated to savings and investments. This part is crucial for building your future wealth and ensuring financial security.

Ten percent of your income can be used for personal enjoyment and discretionary spending. It is important to enjoy the fruits of your labour, but in moderation.

When I first applied this rule, it helped me streamline my budget and prioritize my financial goals. It also made it clearer where I could cut back and how much I could comfortably invest each month.

Debt Assessment:
Understanding your debt is crucial. Identify 'good debt', like a mortgage or student loans, versus 'bad debt', like high-interest credit cards. Prioritize paying off high-interest debt first, as it eats into your ability to save and invest. I tackled my credit card debt by switching to a card with a lower interest rate and setting up a strict payment plan.

Setting Initial Financial Goals:
Finally, set some initial financial goals based on your assessment. These should be SMART: Specific, Measurable, Achievable, Relevant, and Time-bound. My first goal was to build an emergency fund that covered six months of living expenses, which gave me a financial buffer and peace of mind.

We have covered a lot in this first chapter, from understanding your financial status to applying the 70:20:10 rule for managing your finances. I encourage you to take the time now to complete your own financial self-assessment. It is the first real step towards becoming an informed and empowered investor. Remember, every great journey starts with understanding where you are today.

CHAPTER 2: BUDGETING FOR SUCCESS

In this chapter, we dive deep into the essential skill of budgeting, which is not just about making ends meet—it is about making smart decisions that allow you to enjoy life while securing your financial future. With the help of some current UK financial statistics, I, Alex, will show you how to manage your finances effectively to enjoy both your present and future.

The Importance of a Realistic Budget:
Budgeting is not just about restriction; it is a strategic approach to your life and your choices. As someone who loves traveling and social outings, I have learned to create a budget that accommodates these interests without compromising my financial goals.

UK Buying Habits and Financial Overview:
Recent studies indicate that the average monthly pay for young adults in the UK is approximately £2,000 after taxes. However, spending habits show a significant portion of income goes towards dining out, online shopping, and entertainment. Recognizing these trends is crucial in understanding how to allocate your budget effectively.

Step-by-Step Guide to Creating Your Budget:

List Your Income Sources: Start with what you earn monthly, which for our example will be the average £2,000.
Determine Fixed Expenses: Typically, these include rent (£700), utilities (£150), and transportation (£100).
Set Aside for Savings and Investments: Applying the 70:20:10 rule, you should allocate 20%, which is £400, to your savings and investments.
Account for Variable Expenses: This includes groceries (£250), dining out (£100), and other variable costs.
Prioritize Discretionary Spending: With the remaining £300, budget for your

The Millennial Investor: Simple Strategies for Long-Term Wealth.

personal enjoyment like holidays and nights out, ensuring these expenditures do not undermine your financial stability.

Using Tools and Apps to Help:

To keep everything on track, use budgeting apps like Emma, which categorizes your spending and helps track where your money goes. For a seamless banking experience, Monzo offers budgeting tools and instant spending notifications, making it easier to manage your money effectively.

Adjusting Your Budget Over Time:

Your financial situation will change, and so should your budget. Whether it is a salary increase, a new expense, or a change in financial goals, regular reviews are essential. I recommend adjusting your budget every six months to ensure it meets your current needs and future goals.

Effective budgeting is the GPS for your financial journey. It not only guides your spending and saving but also ensures that you reach your destination—financial independence while enjoying a fulfilling life. Remember, incorporating your passions, such as traveling and socializing, into your budget makes it sustainable and enjoyable.

CHAPTER 3: EMERGENCY FUNDS AND FINANCIAL SAFETY

Building a robust financial safety net is crucial, and that is what an emergency fund is all about. In this chapter, I, Alex, will share a personal story that underscores the critical role an emergency fund plays in financial planning.

The Importance of an Emergency Fund:
An emergency fund acts as your financial shock absorber against life's unpredictable bumps. It is designed to help you manage financial stress caused by unexpected expenses without derailing your regular budget or pushing you into debt.

Alex's Story:
Early in my career, I was overly confident with my steady income and minimal savings, believing I could handle any financial surprises. However, life had other plans. Just two months after using most of my savings to buy a car, I faced a sudden job layoff. Without a comprehensive emergency fund, I found it incredibly challenging to cover daily expenses and bills. It was a period filled with stress and uncertainty that could have been mitigated with better financial preparation.

Learning from Experience:
This experience was a wake-up call. I realized the importance of being prepared for the worst while hoping for the best, leading me to prioritize building an emergency fund. Here is how I started, and what I recommend:

How Much Should You Save?

Rule of Thumb: Aim for three to six months' worth of living expenses. This range is standard advice, but your specific savings goal may vary depending on your living situation.

The Millennial Investor: Simple Strategies for Long-Term Wealth.

Adapting to Your Circumstances: If, for example, you are living with parents and have lower expenses, you might find it an opportune time to save or invest even more. Conversely, if you have high fixed expenses or dependents, consider aiming towards the upper end of the scale.

Strategies for Building Your Emergency Fund:

Start Small: Begin by saving a small percentage of your income, gradually increasing as you adjust your spending habits.

Automate Your Savings: Automation ensures you consistently save without having to think about it each month. Set up a direct transfer to a savings account each payday.

Keep it Separate but Accessible: Store your emergency fund in a high-interest savings account that remains separate from your regular checking account to avoid the temptation to spend it yet is accessible without penalties if needed.

Maintaining Your Emergency Fund:

Regular Reviews: Annually adjust your fund in relation to your current living expenses to ensure it still covers your needs.

Purposeful Use: Use this fund strictly for emergencies. Casual withdrawals for non-urgent spending can leave you exposed when a real crisis hits.

Using Tools to Help Manage Your Fund:

Apps like Monzo and Emma are excellent for monitoring your emergency funds. They provide alerts if your balance drops and help you stay on track with your financial goals.

My experience taught me that an emergency fund is not just a nice-to-have; it is essential for maintaining peace of mind. By setting up and diligently maintaining this fund, you will be well-prepared for life's uncertainties.

CHAPTER 4: DEBT MANAGEMENT

Debt can be a significant barrier to financial freedom and a source of constant stress. In this chapter, we will explore how to manage and reduce your debts strategically. I will, Alex, share practical tips and personal experiences that have helped me, and many others regain control over our financial lives.

Understanding Different Types of Debt:

Good Debt vs. Bad Debt: Learn to distinguish between debts that can potentially increase your net worth or have future value (like a mortgage or student loans) and those that do not (like credit card debt).
Interest Rates and Terms: Understanding the interest rates and repayment terms is crucial for prioritizing which debts to pay off first.
Alex's Approach to Debt Management:
When I found myself struggling with various debts, I realized that not all debts are created equal. Here is how I tackled them:

List All Your Debts: Start by listing all your debts, including the creditor, total amount of debt, interest rate, and monthly payment. This visibility is crucial for the next steps.
Prioritize High-Interest Debts: I used the avalanche method, which focuses on paying off debts with the highest interest rates first. This approach saves you money on interest over time.
Consider Debt Consolidation: If you are juggling multiple high-interest debts, consider a consolidation loan. I consolidated my credit card debts into one loan with a lower interest rate, which made them easier and cheaper to manage.
Creating a Debt Reduction Plan:

Budget for Repayments: Adjust your budget to prioritize debt repayment. This might mean reducing discretionary spending or finding ways to increase your income.

Set Clear Goals: Establish clear, achievable goals for debt reduction. For example, aim to pay off your highest interest debt within a year.

Regular Monitoring and Adjustment: Keep track of your progress and adjust your plan as needed. Celebrating small victories along the way can provide motivation.

Alex's Tips for Staying Out of Debt:

Avoid New Debt: Resist the temptation to take on new debt. If you need to make a large purchase, plan and save for it rather than relying on credit.

Emergency Fund: As discussed in the previous chapter, having an emergency fund is crucial. It prevents you from falling back into debt when unexpected expenses arise.

Using Tools to Help Manage Your Debt:

Financial apps and websites can provide valuable assistance in managing your debt. Tools like Debt Payoff Planner and Unbury. Me offer helpful visualizations of your debts and repayment progress.

Managing debt is not just about making payments; it is about strategic planning and consistent effort. With the right approach, you can reduce your debt, minimize interest costs, and move closer to financial freedom.

CHAPTER 5: SAVINGS STRATEGIES

Saving effectively is foundational to achieving both financial security and specific personal goals. In this chapter, we will explore various strategies to maximize your savings potential, ensuring you can meet both short-term needs and long-term aspirations. I am Alex, and I will share my journey and techniques that have significantly boosted my financial growth through disciplined saving practices.

Understanding Savings Goals:
Setting clear and structured savings goals is essential for effective financial planning. These goals can generally be divided into two types: short-term and long-term.

Short-Term Goals: These are immediate needs you expect to pay for within the next few years, such as an emergency fund, a holiday, or a new laptop. The priority here is liquidity and safety, ensuring funds are accessible without risking the principal amount.
Long-Term Goals: These involve larger sums and a longer time horizon, such as saving for a house deposit, your children's education, or your own retirement. Investments for these goals typically carry higher risks but offer greater returns, leveraging the power of compound interest over time.
Setting SMART Goals:
To ensure your savings plan is effective, set SMART goals:

Specific: Clearly define what each goal will fund.
Measurable: Determine how much money is needed.
Achievable: Ensure you can realistically save the required amount given your income and expenses.
Relevant: Make sure the goals are important to your long-term financial health and personal happiness.
Time-bound: Assign a deadline for achieving each goal to stay on track.

The Millennial Investor: Simple Strategies for Long-Term Wealth.

Alex's Perspective on the Importance of Budgeting

Budgeting has always been a cornerstone of my financial strategy, both personally and professionally. It is the tool through which I navigate my finances, ensuring not only stability but also enabling the realization of my financial goals. From the outset of my career, I recognized the significance of a well-structured budget in maintaining financial health and fostering wealth accumulation.

The Foundation of Financial Control

For me, budgeting is not merely about tracking expenses or cutting costs—it is about creating a clear roadmap for financial decision-making. It allows me to allocate resources efficiently, prioritize expenditures, and monitor my financial progress. Without a budget, managing my finances would be like navigating a road trip without a map.

Setting and Achieving Financial Goals

One of the most critical functions of budgeting in my life has been its role in goal setting. Whether it is saving for a down payment on a property, investing in stocks, or setting aside money for retirement, a budget is the framework that makes these goals attainable. By delineating how much money I direct towards each goal, I can balance my short-term desires with my long-term objectives, ensuring that I do not sacrifice one for the other.

Adapting to Financial Changes

Budgeting has also been instrumental in adapting to financial changes over the years. Whether it was a change in income levels, unexpected expenses, or economic downturns, having a flexible budget allowed me to adjust quickly and efficiently. This adaptability has been crucial in maintaining financial stability during uncertain times.

Tools and Techniques

I utilize a variety of tools to keep my budgeting precise and effective. Spreadsheet software has been my go-to for many years, allowing me to customize my budget categories and track my monthly cash flow meticulously. More recently, I have integrated budgeting apps that link directly to my financial accounts, providing real-time tracking of expenditures and alerts that help me stay on course.

Educating Others on Budgeting

Given the benefits I have experienced, I am a strong advocate for budgeting and often find myself advising friends, family, and mentees on setting up their budgets. I emphasize starting simple: differentiate between needs and wants, understand your income streams, and make sure your expenses do not exceed your income. From there, it is about refining and adjusting as you go.

The Millennial Investor: Simple Strategies for Long-Term Wealth.

Overall, budgeting has been more than just a financial tool for me—it is a lifestyle choice that has provided me with freedom rather than restriction. It has given me peace of mind knowing that I am in control of my finances and am making informed decisions that will benefit my current financial situation and my financial future. For anyone looking to improve their financial health, I cannot recommend budgeting highly enough. It is the first step towards financial empowerment and a cornerstone of a sound financial plan...

Choosing the Right Savings Accounts:
Different financial goals require different types of savings accounts:

High-Interest Savings Accounts: Ideal for short-term goals due to their higher interest rates compared to regular savings accounts.
ISAs (Individual Savings Accounts): In the UK, these accounts offer tax-free saving and investing. They are incredibly effective for both short-term and long-term goals, given their flexibility and tax advantages.
Certificates of Deposit and Bonds: Suitable for medium to long-term goals, these offer fixed returns over a predetermined period and are generally safer than stocks.

Understanding and setting clear savings goals, coupled with selecting the appropriate savings vehicles, are critical steps toward achieving financial stability and realizing your personal dreams. My experience with ISAs demonstrates how structured saving and investing can significantly accelerate financial growth and provide substantial benefits in the long run.

Section 2: The Importance of Wealth Growth

CHAPTER 6: THE POWER OF COMPOUNDING

Compounding interest is one of the most powerful forces in finance, capable of transforming modest savings into substantial wealth over time. In this chapter, I, Alex, will delve into how compounding works and demonstrate its profound impact on long-term investment success.

Understanding Compounding Interest:
Compounding interest is the process where the value of an investment grows exponentially over time because the returns themselves earn interest. This concept is best summarized by Albert Einstein's famous quote, describing compounding interest as the "eighth wonder of the world."

Illustrative Example of Compounding:
Let us say you start with £1,000 in an investment account that earns 5% annual interest. Here is how your investment grows over time due to compounding:

Year 1: £1,000 + 5% = £1,050
Year 2: £1,050 + 5% = £1,102.50
Year 3: £1,102.50 + 5% = £1,157.63
Over 30 years, this initial £1,000 grows to over £4,321.94 without any additional contributions, purely through the power of compounding.

The Rule of 72:
A quick way to estimate how long it will take for an investment to double using compounding is the Rule of seventy-two. Simply divide seventy-two by your expected annual interest rate. For example, at an 8% return rate, your investment will double every 9 years (72 / 8 = 9).

The Millennial Investor: Simple Strategies for Long-Term Wealth.

Strategies to Maximize Compounding:

Start Early: The sooner you start investing, the more significant the benefits of compounding due to the longer growth period.
Regular Contributions: Consistently adding to your investments increases the base amount that compounds, accelerating growth.
Reinvest Earnings: Automatically reinvest dividends and interest payments to further enhance the compounding effect.
Avoid Withdrawals: Try not to withdraw from your investments, as this reduces the principal amount that benefits from compounding.
Alex's Personal Experience with Compounding:
I started investing in a diversified portfolio of stocks and bonds in my early twenties. By consistently reinvesting dividends and interest, and making regular contributions, I have watched my portfolio grow exponentially. It was compounding that enabled me to achieve financial independence much earlier than expected.

Common Misconceptions about Compounding:

It is Only for Rich People: You do not need a lot of money to benefit from compounding; what you need is time and consistency.
It is Too Late to Start: It is never too late to benefit from compounding. While starting earlier is better, starting now is better than not starting at all.
Using Compounding in Debt Management:
Compounding is not just for investments; it also applies to debt. Understanding how compounding interest on your debt can accelerate your financial burden is crucial. This realization can motivate you to prioritize paying off high-interest debts quickly.

The power of compounding is a fundamental principle that every investor should understand and utilize. Whether you are saving for retirement, a down payment on a house, or your child's education, embracing the principles of compounding can help you reach your financial goals more efficiently and effectively. Remember, when it comes to compounding, time is your greatest ally.

CHAPTER 7: INTRODUCTION TO INVESTING VEHICLES

Investing is an essential tool for building wealth over the long term. In this chapter, I, Alex, will cover the fundamental concepts that every young investor should understand before embarking on their investment journey.

What is Investing?
Investing involves committing money to an endeavour with the expectation of achieving a profit over time. This typically includes buying stocks, bonds, mutual funds, or real estate with the aim that the asset will grow in value or produce income.

Why Invest?
The primary reason to invest is to ensure your money grows faster than it would in a savings account, particularly in an environment where inflation can decrease the purchasing power of money. Investing is key to achieving financial goals like retirement, buying a home, or funding education.

The Millennial Investor: Simple Strategies for Long-Term Wealth.

Types of Investments:

Stocks: Shares of ownership in a company. Stocks are well-known for their potential for high returns, but they also come with higher risks.

Bonds: Loans investors make to corporations or governments in exchange for periodic interest payments plus the return of the bond's face value at maturity. Bonds are generally considered safer than stocks.

Mutual Funds: Investments that pool money from many investors to purchase a diversified portfolio of stocks and/or bonds. Mutual funds offer diversification and professional management.

Real Estate: Property consisting of land and the buildings on it. Real estate can provide income through renting and potential appreciation in property value.

Exchange-Traded Funds (ETFs): Similar to mutual funds, but ETFs trade on stock exchanges much like ordinary stocks. They offer low expense ratios and tax efficiency.

Investment Risk and Return:

Every investment comes with its own set of risks, which are closely tied to its potential returns. Generally, higher-risk investments offer the potential for higher returns:

Market Risk: The risk of investments losing value because of economic developments or other events that affect the entire market.

Credit Risk: The risk that a government entity or company that issued the bond will run into financial difficulties and will not be able to pay the interest or repay the principal at maturity.

Interest Rate Risk: The risk that an investment's value will change due to a change in the absolute level of interest rates, in the spread between two rates, or in any other interest rate relationship.

How to Start Investing:

Set Clear Goals: Define what you are saving for and your time horizon. This will help determine your investment strategy.

Understand Your Risk Tolerance: Assess how much risk you are willing to take and what types of investments match your risk profile.

The Millennial Investor: Simple Strategies for Long-Term Wealth.

Start Small: You do not need a lot of money to start investing. Many platforms allow you to buy fractional shares or invest small amounts in mutual funds or ETFs.

Diversify: Do not put all your eggs in one basket. Diversification helps reduce your risk by spreading your investment across various asset classes.

Review and Adjust: Regularly review your investment portfolio to ensure it aligns with your goals and adjust as needed based on changes in your life circumstances or financial markets.

Alex's Experience with Investing Basics
When I first ventured into the world of investing, my initial focus was primarily on stocks due to their high return potential. This decision was driven by the attractive prospects of capital growth that stocks historically offer. Eager to capitalize on these opportunities, I immersed myself in studying market trends and individual stock performances, aiming to build a portfolio that would yield substantial returns.

Initial Focus on Stocks
My early investment strategy was straightforward: identify high-growth stocks that could provide significant returns over time. I was particularly drawn to tech stocks, which seemed poised for exponential growth. The thrill of potentially striking big with these investments was exhilarating at first. However, as I became more immersed in the realities of stock trading, I encountered the inherent volatility of the stock market.

Learning from Volatility
The stock market is as unpredictable as it is potentially lucrative. I experienced my first major market downturn not long after starting my investment journey. This period of significant volatility was a stark reminder of the risks involved in stock investing. Watching the value of my carefully selected stocks fluctuate wildly taught me an invaluable lesson about the importance of risk management in an investment portfolio.

Embracing Diversification
This experience led me to rethink my investment strategy. I realized that while stocks are essential for growth, having a diversified portfolio could stabilize returns and reduce overall risk. To achieve this balance, I began to explore other asset classes, specifically bonds and real estate.

Incorporating Bonds:
I added bonds to my portfolio to provide a steady income stream and

The Millennial Investor: Simple Strategies for Long-Term Wealth.

counterbalance the volatility of stocks. Bonds, with their regular interest payments and principal security at maturity, offered a much-needed cushion against the ups and downs of the stock market.

Investing in Real Estate:
Real estate investment was another strategic move to diversify my holdings. Real estate can provide both rental income and long-term capital appreciation, making it a valuable component of a diversified investment portfolio. Additionally, the physical nature of real estate as an asset provides a tangible security that stocks and bonds cannot.

The Impact of Diversification
By diversifying my portfolio to include stocks, bonds, and real estate, I managed to create a more resilient investment strategy. This diversification not only reduced the risk but also smoothed out the returns over time, providing a more stable financial growth path. Each asset class played a different role: stocks for growth, bonds for income and stability, and real estate for tangible asset appreciation and rental yields.

My initial foray into investing, primarily focused on stocks, taught me the hard lessons of market volatility. These experiences shaped my approach to investing, underscoring the critical importance of diversification. By expanding my portfolio to include bonds and real estate, I was able to mitigate risk and achieve a more balanced and stable return on my investments. This holistic approach has been fundamental in building a robust financial foundation that can withstand market fluctuations and support my long-term financial goals.

Understanding the basics of investing is crucial for anyone looking to build wealth. By investing wisely, you can grow your financial resources, achieve your financial goals, and secure your financial future. Remember, the key to successful investing is not just about choosing the right assets but also managing risks and continually learning and adapting to new information.

CHAPTER 8: PLANNING FOR RETIREMENT EARLY

Starting early with retirement planning is not just advantageous; it is essential for building a comfortable future. In this chapter, I, Alex, will break down why early retirement planning is crucial, and I will provide actionable strategies to maximize your retirement savings. Understanding the power of time and compounding can transform modest savings into substantial sums by the time you retire.

Why Start Early?

1. Compound Interest:

Explanation: The sooner you start saving, the more time your money has to grow through compound interest. Small, regular investments can grow exponentially over decades, thanks to the returns generating their own returns. Example: If you start saving £200 a month at 25 with an average annual return of 7%, you will have around £525,000 by age 65. If you start at 35, you will have about £244,000, less than half of what you could have saved by starting earlier.

2. Lower Lifetime Contribution:

Benefit: By starting earlier, you can contribute less money overall but end up with more in the end. This is because the longer your investment horizon, the harder your money works for you.

The Millennial Investor: Simple Strategies for Long-Term Wealth.

Impact: This not only makes it less financially stressful on a month-to-month basis but also allows for more flexible financial decisions throughout your life.

3. Increased Investment Opportunities:

Advantage: An early start in investing gives you the latitude to take on riskier (potentially higher return) investments since you have time to recover from any downturns in the market.
Strategic Approach: Younger investors can allocate a larger portion of their portfolio to equities and gradually shift to more conservative investments as they approach retirement.

Strategies for Effective Retirement Planning

1. Take Advantage of Workplace Pensions:

Auto-enrolment: In the UK, employers must automatically enrol eligible employees into a workplace pension. Contributions are made by both the employee and employer, which can significantly enhance retirement savings.
Maximizing Contributions: Try to contribute the maximum amount that your employer will match, as this is essentially free money and boosts your pension pot.

2. Open a Personal Pension Plan:

SIPP (Self-Invested Personal Pension): SIPPs offer more control over your investment choices compared to traditional personal pensions. They are suitable for those who are comfortable making their own investment decisions.
Benefits: Tax relief on contributions, with the government adding basic rate tax relief directly to your pension.

3. Explore ISAs for Additional Savings:

Lifetime ISA (LISA): Specifically useful for younger individuals, offering a 25% bonus on contributions up to £4,000 per year, which can be used towards retirement.

Flexibility and Access: Unlike pensions, money saved in ISAs can be accessed before retirement age, offering flexibility in case of emergencies.

4. Regular Reviews and Adjustments:

Keeping Track: Regularly review your retirement plans to ensure they are on track to meet your goals. This includes assessing your investment performance, contribution levels, and any changes in your financial situation. Adjusting Portfolio: As you move closer to retirement, shift your investment strategy to focus more on income and preservation of capital to reduce exposure to market volatility.

Alex's Experience with Early Retirement Planning
From the onset of my career, I recognized the importance of early retirement planning. Understanding the power of compound interest and the benefits of starting young, I began contributing to my pension as soon as I received my first pay check. This foundational decision set the stage for a disciplined approach to securing financial independence well before the traditional retirement age.

Commitment to Pension Contributions
I made it a priority to contribute to my pension regularly, treating it as a non-negotiable expense. This early and consistent investment in my pension was a strategic move based on the principle that small, regular savings can accumulate to significant amounts over time due to compound interest. Whenever I received a raise, I increased my pension contributions proportionally. This strategy allowed me to progressively grow my retirement fund while maintaining my standard of living, ensuring that each salary increment also bolstered my future financial security.

Leveraging a Lifetime ISA (LISA)
In addition to my pension, I opened a Lifetime ISA to take full advantage of government incentives. The LISA offered a 25% bonus on contributions up to £4,000 each year, which presented an incredible opportunity to accelerate my savings. I used the LISA as a complementary fund to my pension, dedicating it towards additional retirement savings or as a potential fund for purchasing my first home. The flexibility of the LISA made it an invaluable tool in my broader retirement strategy.

Setting Retirement Capital Goals
My goal has always been to achieve a level of capital that would not only sustain my lifestyle in retirement but also provide the freedom to pursue passions without financial constraints. To this end, I calculated that I would need a retirement fund that could support approximately 70% of my final working salary annually. This would allow me to maintain a comfortable lifestyle while accommodating for inflation and potential healthcare needs.

Based on current projections and my savings rate, I aim to accumulate a retirement pot of around £1 million by the age of fifty-five. This target is ambitious but achievable with my savings strategy, which includes maximizing pension contributions, leveraging the LISA, and making prudent investment choices to ensure my savings grow efficiently over the decades.

The Benefits of Early Planning
The advantages of starting my retirement planning early have been manifold. Not only have I been able to benefit from compound interest and government bonuses, but I have also instilled a sense of financial discipline in my daily life that extends beyond just saving for retirement. This discipline has allowed me to make informed and strategic financial decisions consistently, reducing stress and increasing my overall financial literacy.

My experience with early retirement planning emphasizes the importance of starting as early as possible and taking advantage of any available financial tools, such as pensions and LISAs. By setting clear goals and consistently adhering to a strategic saving plan, I am on track to secure a financially stable and fulfilling retirement, well ahead of the traditional timeline. This proactive approach has not only prepared me financially for the future but also provided peace of mind that my later years will be secure and enjoyable.

Starting your retirement planning early can make a monumental difference in your financial security later in life. It allows you to take full advantage of compounding, reduce the stress of large contributions later on, and provides more opportunities to grow your investment. By strategically planning and regularly reviewing your retirement goals, you can ensure a stable and comfortable retirement.

CHAPTER 9: REAL ESTATE AS AN INVESTMENT

Investing in real estate is a proven strategy for building wealth, offering not only the potential for capital appreciation but also the opportunity to generate passive income. In this chapter, I, Alex, will guide you through the nuances of real estate investment, focusing on strategies that are particularly accessible to young investors in the UK. We will examine the robust rental market, the profitability of property flipping, and the overall benefits of investing in real estate.

Understanding the UK Real Estate Market
Rental Market Dynamics:

Demand for Rentals: According to recent studies, approximately 20% of UK households are in the private rental sector, and this number is expected to rise. High demand in urban areas, especially in cities like London, Manchester, and Birmingham, highlights significant income potential for landlords.

Income Potential: The average rental yield in the UK can vary widely by location, with yields in the North of England often exceeding 7%, while areas in South and Central London may see lower yields around 3% to 4%.

Flipping Properties for Profit:

Market Trends: The property flipping market in the UK remains lucrative, with average profits on a single flipped property standing around £30,000. However, profits can be significantly higher in high-demand areas, particularly when renovations substantially improve a property's appeal.

Considerations: Successful flipping requires an understanding of purchase costs, renovation budgets, and the after-repair value (ARV). Market timing and speed of renovation are also critical to maximizing return on investment.

The Millennial Investor: Simple Strategies for Long-Term Wealth.

Real Estate Investment Strategies for Young Investors

1. House Hacking:

Concept: This involves purchasing a multi-unit property, living in one unit, and renting out the others. It is an excellent way for young investors to enter the market while offsetting their own housing costs.
Benefits: This strategy not only helps in reducing personal living expenses but also in gaining firsthand management experience.

2. Buy-to-Let Investments:

Strategy: Investing in property specifically to rent it out. With the rental demand high, especially among millennials and young professionals, this strategy offers a consistent income stream.

ROI Considerations: Investors need to factor in costs such as mortgage payments, property maintenance, and potential periods of vacancy. However, with strategic location choices and good property management, the returns can be highly favourable.

3. Real Estate Crowdfunding:

Introduction: Crowdfunding platforms allow investors to start with smaller amounts of capital, investing in properties collectively with other investors.
Advantage: This method offers exposure to larger, potentially more profitable real estate projects traditionally accessible only to more affluent investors.

4. Property Flipping:

Approach: Focus on buying undervalued properties in areas with high growth potential, renovate them, and sell for a profit.

Key Stats: The success of flipping relies heavily on market knowledge and renovation expertise. The average time to flip a house is about six months, and the profit margin can increase substantially with well-planned renovations.

Alex's Experience with Real Estate Investments
In my broader investment portfolio, real estate has played a pivotal role, offering both challenges and substantial rewards. One of my earliest and most educational experiences came from flipping my first property—a small flat in the UK. This venture not only provided practical insights into the real estate market but also tested my resilience and adaptability as an investor.

The Millennial Investor: Simple Strategies for Long-Term Wealth.

The First Flip: A Small Flat in the UK

The property was a modest flat located in an up-and-coming neighbourhood known for its potential for growth. My initial attraction to this flat stemmed from its relatively low purchase price and the opportunity it presented for significant value addition through renovations.

The Renovation Process:

The renovation process was both challenging and enlightening. It involved updating the kitchen and bathroom, overhauling the living space to create a more open and inviting environment, and modernizing the fixtures and fittings to appeal to contemporary tastes. Each step required careful planning, budget management, and coordination with contractors and suppliers.

Challenges Encountered:

One of the main challenges was staying within budget. Unexpected costs arose, particularly with structural issues that were not apparent during the initial inspection. Navigating these financial surprises tested my problem-solving skills and financial management. Additionally, the project timeline extended beyond my initial estimates, primarily due to delays in supply chains and contractor availability.

Rewards and Learning Points:

Despite the challenges, the rewards of flipping this property were significant. Upon completion of the renovations, the flat's market value had increased substantially, allowing me to sell it at a considerable profit. This successful flip not only provided a financial boost but also invaluable lessons in real estate investment, such as the importance of thorough due diligence, the benefits of building a reliable team, and the need for flexibility in timelines and budgeting.

This experience underscored the importance of resilience and adaptability, especially when dealing with the unpredictability of real estate renovations. The ability to swiftly respond to unforeseen challenges and adjust plans accordingly was crucial for the success of the project.

Flipping my first property was a landmark experience in my investment career. It taught me critical aspects of real estate investment and property management, from the tactical skills needed to efficiently renovate and flip a property to the strategic patience required to wait for the right selling moment. Each step of the journey provided insights that I have carried into subsequent real estate ventures, continuously refining my approach to maximize both the financial rewards and personal satisfaction derived from transforming properties.

Real estate remains a formidable sector for investment, with the UK market

The Millennial Investor: Simple Strategies for Long-Term Wealth.

offering numerous opportunities for young investors. Whether it is generating passive income through rental properties or realizing capital gains through property flipping, the key to success is understanding market dynamics and managing investments wisely. Remember, real estate not only diversifies your investment portfolio but also provides a tangible asset that can serve as a long-term wealth-building tool.

CHAPTER 10: ALTERNATIVE INVESTMENTS

As financial markets evolve, so do the opportunities for diversification beyond traditional stocks and bonds. In this chapter, I, Alex, will introduce you to the world of alternative investments, which can include everything from cryptocurrencies to private equity. We will explore the unique benefits and risks of these non-conventional assets, and I will provide guidance on how they can fit into a well-rounded investment portfolio.

Understanding Alternative Investments

Definition and Scope:

Alternative Investments: These are investments in assets that do not conform to the standard categories of stocks, bonds, or cash. These types of investments are known for their complexity, exclusivity, and potential to enhance portfolio diversification.

Types of Alternative Investments:

Private Equity and Venture Capital:

Overview: Investments in companies not publicly traded on the stock exchange. Private equity involves investing directly in private companies, while venture capital focuses on early-stage, high-potential startups.
Benefits: Potential for substantial returns if the companies grow or go public.
Risks: High risk due to the potential for company failure, illiquidity, and longer investment horizons required for returns.

Hedge Funds:

Overview: Pooled investment funds that employ different strategies to earn

active returns, or alpha, for their investors.
Benefits: Potential to generate returns in both rising and falling markets through strategies such as leverage, derivatives, and short selling.
Risks: Complex strategies that often come with higher fees and greater risk of significant losses.

Real Assets:

Types: Tangible assets like real estate, commodities, and natural resources.
Benefits: Provide a hedge against inflation and are less sensitive to stock market fluctuations.
Risks: Can be highly volatile depending on economic factors; physical assets require maintenance and have costs associated with them.

Cryptocurrencies:

Overview: Digital or virtual currencies that use cryptography for security.
Benefits: High growth potential and independence from traditional financial systems.
Risks: Extreme volatility and uncertain regulatory environment.

Incorporating Alternative Investments into Your Portfolio

Strategic Considerations:

Diversification: By adding alternative investments to a portfolio, investors can reduce risk through diversification, as these assets often behave differently than traditional stocks and bonds.
Allocation: It is generally advised to allocate a smaller portion of your portfolio to alternative investments due to their higher risk and complexity.
Assessing Suitability:

Investor Profile: Suitable for investors with a higher risk tolerance, longer investment horizons, and those who have a significant base of traditional investments.

Due Diligence: Essential due to the complexity and lower transparency of many alternative investments compared to traditional assets.

Alex's Experience with Alternative Investments
Throughout my investment journey, I have continually sought opportunities beyond the traditional stocks and bonds to diversify my portfolio and tap into new sources of growth. My exploration into alternative investments has been particularly rewarding and enlightening.

Venture Capital Through Crowdfunding

One of the more adventurous facets of my investment strategy has been my foray into venture capital via crowdfunding platforms, specifically those focusing on tech startups. This approach has allowed me to directly invest in a variety of promising tech companies at an early stage. Platforms like SeedInvest and Kickstarter have been instrumental in providing access to these opportunities, which are typically reserved for institutional investors.

The potential for high returns in this sector is significant, given the explosive growth potential of tech startups. However, the risks are equally high, as many startups do not succeed. To mitigate these risks, I perform thorough due diligence on each potential investment, examining the business model, the experience and expertise of the founding team, and the product's market potential.

Investing in Real Assets

In addition to venture capital, I have allocated a portion of my portfolio to real assets, particularly precious metals like gold and silver. These investments serve as a hedge against inflation and market volatility. In times of economic uncertainty, when traditional stocks and bonds may falter, precious metals typically hold or increase their value.

I manage these investments through commodities exchanges and specialized investment funds that focus on precious metals. This strategy not only provides a safety net for my portfolio but also balances the high-risk nature of my venture capital investments.

Balancing High Risk with Stability

This dual approach of investing in high-risk tech startups and stable precious metals allows me to balance my portfolio's risk and return effectively. The excitement and potential high returns of venture capital investments in tech startups offer the possibility of significant growth, while the stability of precious metals provides a dependable buffer against potential losses.

My experience with alternative investments has taught me the importance of diversification not just across sectors but also across different types of investment vehicles. By branching out into venture capital through crowdfunding and investing in tangible assets like precious metals, I have not only spread my risks but also enhanced my potential for higher returns. Each investment decision comes with its set of challenges and learning curves, and navigating these has been an integral part of my growth as an investor.

Alternative investments can enhance portfolio diversification and potentially boost returns, but they come with their own set of risks and complexities. For those prepared to navigate these waters, the rewards can be significant, offering opportunities that are not tied to the conventional financial markets. As always, understanding your own financial goals and risk tolerance is key to deciding if and how to incorporate these investments into your strategy.

Section 3: Investing in the Stock Market

The Millennial Investor: Simple Strategies for Long-Term Wealth.

CHAPTER 11: STOCK MARKET BASICS

The stock market is a critical engine of economic growth, offering opportunities for companies to raise capital and for investors to secure financial returns. In this chapter, I, Alex, will explore the intricacies of the stock market, including its operation, the significance of tracking historical trends, and the performance of major indices compared to UK inflation rates. We will also discuss the role of accessible trading platforms like Trading 212 and eToro, which have democratized investing by making market participation more user-friendly.

Basics of the Stock Market

The Millennial Investor: Simple Strategies for Long-Term Wealth.

What is the Stock Market?

Definition: The stock market encompasses various exchanges, such as the London Stock Exchange (LSE) and the New York Stock Exchange (NYSE), where ownership shares of public companies are bought and sold. These exchanges facilitate liquidity and price discovery for stocks listed on the market.

Functions of the Stock Market:

Capital Raising: Companies issue shares to raise funds for various needs, including expansion, innovation, and debt management, fostering economic development.

Investment Opportunities: The stock market offers investors the chance to own a portion of a company, with potential returns through dividends and capital gains.

Key Concepts in Stock Market Investing

Shares and Dividends:

Shares: Represent equity ownership in a company, with shareholders benefiting financially from the company's success.
Dividends: Periodic payments made out of profits to shareholders, providing an income stream from their investment.

Market Indices and Inflation:

Major Indices: The FTSE 100, for instance, tracks the performance of the top one hundred companies on the LSE and is used as an indicator of the overall market health.

Historical Performance vs. Inflation: Historically, the FTSE 100 has offered returns of around 6-8% annually, surpassing the UK's average inflation rate of 2-3%. This demonstrates the stock market's potential to deliver growth that exceeds inflation, enhancing the purchasing power of long-term investors.

Bull and Bear Markets:

Bull Market: Characterized by rising stock prices, occurring in times of strong economic performance and investor confidence.
Bear Market: Defined by falling stock prices, often triggered by economic recessions or widespread pessimistic outlooks among investors.

Getting Started with Stock Investments

The Millennial Investor: Simple Strategies for Long-Term Wealth.

1. Setting Up a Brokerage Account:

Platforms like Trading 212 and eToro: These platforms offer user-friendly interfaces, low transaction fees, and the ability to buy fractional shares, making it easier for beginners to start investing. They also provide educational resources to help new investors understand market dynamics.

2. Making Your First Investment:

Research and Diversification: It is crucial to research potential investments thoroughly and to diversify your portfolio across different sectors to mitigate risk.

Using Apps: Apps like Trading 212 and eToro not only facilitate easy trading but also offer tools for tracking portfolio performance and market trends, helping investors make informed decisions.

3. Investment Strategies:

Buy and Hold vs. Active Trading: Depending on your risk tolerance and investment horizon, you may choose a long-term, buy-and-hold strategy, or engage in more active trading to capitalize on market fluctuations.

Alex's Insights on Navigating the Stock Market

Navigating the stock market has been an integral part of my investment journey, combining a keen analysis of historical market data with the strategic use of cutting-edge technological tools. Platforms like eToro and Trading 212 have been crucial in this process, enabling me to adopt sophisticated trading strategies while keeping costs low.

Leveraging Technology and Historical Data

My approach has always leaned heavily on the blend of deep historical insights and the latest advancements in trading technology. Using platforms like eToro, I have had the opportunity to engage in social trading, where I could follow and replicate the trades of experienced investors. This has been particularly invaluable as a learning tool, allowing me to see firsthand the strategies employed by seasoned traders in real-time.

Trading 212, on the other hand, offered me a sandbox of sorts—a place where I could experiment with small investments across various stocks without the burden of hefty fees. This accessibility made it possible for me to test theories and strategies with minimal financial risk.

Real Investments and Learning from Experience

The Millennial Investor: Simple Strategies for Long-Term Wealth.

Throughout my trading career, I have made several significant investments that have shaped my understanding and strategies. One of my earliest ventures into the stock market was investing in Tesla. Watching the company's stock rise significantly, I realized a substantial profit which solidified my confidence in tech stocks. However, not all investments yielded positive returns. A venture into the pharmaceutical sector, for instance, with a substantial investment in a company that promised but failed to deliver a breakthrough drug, taught me about the volatility and risks inherent in this industry. This loss was a tough but necessary lesson in the importance of diversification and risk management.

Profit and Loss: Learning from Both
One particularly educational instance was during a market downturn, where I experienced significant losses on paper due to a hasty investment in high-risk tech stocks without adequate due diligence. This experience taught me the importance of not following hype and reaffirmed the value of fundamental analysis.

On the other side, one of my most successful investments was in Amazon. By closely monitoring market trends and leveraging data analytics, I bought shares during a dip and saw tremendous growth over the following years, highlighting the benefits of patience and a long-term view in stock investments.

Balancing Strategy with Technology

The stock market can indeed be a potent avenue for financial growth, especially when investors effectively balance traditional investment strategies with modern technological advances. Understanding the historical performance of markets and utilizing innovative trading platforms can significantly enhance one's ability to optimize potential returns while managing risks effectively. My journey through the highs and lows of stock trading has not only bolstered my financial portfolio but also enriched my skills and knowledge, proving indispensable in my continuous quest for financial.

CHAPTER 12: TYPES OF STOCKS

Navigating the stock market and selecting the right stocks can be daunting, especially for novice investors. This chapter, guided by Alex, aims to demystify the process of stock selection by breaking it down into comprehensible components and using straightforward examples. We will explore fundamental and technical analysis and highlight user-friendly tools on platforms like Trading 212 and eToro to make informed decisions more accessible.

Understanding Financial Metrics

1. Earnings and Revenue Growth:

Why It Matters: A company's earnings and revenue are like its heartbeat; steady growth often indicates good health.
Example: If a company reported earnings growth from £1 million to £1.5 million over the past year, it suggests improved profitability, possibly due to increased sales or effective cost management.

2. Profitability Ratios:

Return on Equity (ROE): Shows how well a company uses investment funds to generate earnings growth.
Example: A ROE of 15% means that for every dollar of shareholders' equity, the company generates £0.15 in profit. This is particularly useful when compared to other companies in the same industry.

3. Price-to-Earnings Ratio (P/E):

Explanation: A low P/E ratio may indicate that the stock is undervalued relative to its earnings. Conversely, a high P/E might suggest that it is overvalued—or that investors are expecting high growth rates in the future.

Example: If Company A has a P/E of ten and the industry average is twenty, Company A might be undervalued. This could be a buying opportunity, provided other factors are favourable.

Market and Industry Analysis

1. Sector Trends and Competitive Positioning:

Why It Matters: The sector's health and a company's position within the sector can significantly impact its performance.
Example: In a growing sector like renewable energy, a company that is a leading provider of solar panels might have better long-term prospects than one involved in coal energy.

2. Competitive Advantage (Economic Moat):

Explanation: A moat is what keeps competitors at bay. It could be a proprietary technology, brand reputation, or regulatory barriers.
Example: Apple's brand loyalty is a powerful moat. This loyalty allows it to charge premium prices and maintain high profit margins.

Technical Analysis for Beginners

1. Reading Stock Charts:

Simple Patterns: A 'bullish engulfing' pattern on a candlestick chart suggests that buyers are gaining control, and the price might rise.
Example: If yesterday's stock price opened at £100 and closed at £95 (a down day), but today it opened at £95 and closed at £105 (covering and exceeding the prior day's body), it is a bullish signal.

The Millennial Investor: Simple Strategies for Long-Term Wealth.

2. Moving Averages:

Why They Help: They smooth out price data to identify the trend direction.

Example: If the current price of a stock is above its 50-day moving average, it is generally considered to be in an uptrend, suggesting it might be a good time to buy.

Utilizing Trading Platforms

1. Trading 212 and eToro Features:

Real-Time Data and Simulated Trading: Both platforms offer real-time market data and simulated trading environments, where beginners can practice trading without financial risk.

Social Trading on eToro: This feature allows users to mimic the trades of experienced investors, learning from their strategies and market insights.

2. Practical Application Using Platforms:

Scenario: Imagine you are interested in technology stocks. On eToro, you could follow top traders who specialize in tech investments, see their portfolios, and understand their trading decisions, all of which provide practical insights and learning experiences.

Choosing the right stocks involves a balance of understanding the financial health of companies, recognizing market trends, and utilizing technical indicators. For novices, platforms like Trading 212 and eToro not only provide essential tools and resources but also offer a community and framework where learning is integrated with actual investing experiences. By engaging with these platforms and applying the principles outlined in this chapter, even beginner investors can start to navigate the stock market with confidence and make informed investment choices. Make sure to check out links at the end of the book for any resources we have discussed so far.

CHAPTER 13: FUNDAMENTALS OF TRADING

In today's fast-paced financial markets, the ability to make quick, informed decisions is a critical skill for traders. This chapter, guided by Alex, delves into the essential strategies for developing a decisive trading mindset, employing modern technological tools including AI and advanced analytics to enhance decision-making, and effectively utilizing resources like Yahoo Finance for comprehensive stock research.

Developing a Decisive Trading Mindset

1. Continuous Learning and Emotional Control:

Continuous Learning: The landscape of the market is constantly evolving.

The Millennial Investor: Simple Strategies for Long-Term Wealth.

Staying updated with the latest financial news, technological advancements, and market trends is crucial. Use sights as Udemy and undertake online courses in investing to widen your skill set.

Emotional Control: Successful trading requires managing emotions to avoid impulsive decisions. Techniques such as mindfulness and meditation can help maintain focus and reduce stress.

2. The Role of Artificial Intelligence (AI):

AI in Trading: AI technologies, including algorithms and machine learning models, can analyse vast amounts of market data at speeds and accuracies far beyond human capabilities. Tools like GPT (Generative Pre-trained Transformer) can assist in interpreting complex financial reports, predicting market trends, and providing personalized trading insights.
Practical Use: Incorporating AI tools can enhance traditional trading strategies by providing data-driven insights, thus improving the accuracy of your trading decisions.

Tools and Techniques for Effective Stock Research and Trading

1. Technical and Fundamental Analysis:

Technical Tools: Platforms like Trading 212 offer advanced charting tools that use historical data to predict future price movements.

Fundamental Analysis: Deep dives into financial statements and market positioning are crucial. AI can help synthesize this information into actionable insights, evaluating the health and potential of investments quickly and efficiently.

2. Utilizing Financial News and Data Platforms:

Yahoo Finance: A comprehensive tool for tracking real-time stock data, financial news, and in-depth analysis. It is an essential resource for monitoring your portfolio and potential investments.

AI Integration: AI can help filter and prioritize news on platforms like Yahoo Finance based on your specific interests and past browsing behaviour, enhancing the relevance of the information you receive.

3. Advanced Analytical Tools:

AI-Powered Analysis: Use AI-driven platforms to analyse market sentiments, scan earnings call transcripts, and predict stock volatility. GPT models can generate readable summaries of complex financial data, making it easier to keep up with market changes and opportunities.

Social Trading on eToro: This platform allows you to follow the trading decisions of experienced traders, with AI enhancing the matching process by suggesting traders who match your risk profile and trading goals.

Step-by-Step Guide to Researching and Choosing Stocks

1. Daily and Weekly Routines:

Daily Monitoring: Start the day by checking Yahoo Finance for the latest market trends, significant economic news, and stock movements. Use AI tools to receive personalized news updates.

Weekly Analysis: Allocate time each week for a thorough review of potential stocks using both AI analyses and traditional methods. Compare your findings with industry benchmarks to identify the best opportunities.

2. Real-Time Decision Making:

Trading Platforms: Use real-time trading data and AI suggestions on platforms like Trading 212 to make informed decisions quickly.

Simulations and Forecasts: Employ AI-driven simulations to test potential trading strategies and forecast their outcomes before applying them in real trades.

3. Leveraging AI for Continuous Improvement:

Feedback Loops: Use AI to track the outcomes of your trades and learn from successes and mistakes. AI can identify patterns in your trading behaviour that could be improved.

Decisiveness in trading is significantly enhanced by the strategic use of AI and modern analytics, alongside foundational trading knowledge and emotional intelligence. By leveraging platforms like Yahoo Finance for data-driven insights and embracing AI technologies to process and analyse data, traders can make more informed decisions swiftly. This hybrid approach of human intuition and technological support is the cornerstone of successful modern trading.

CHAPTER 14: RISK MANAGEMENT

Effective risk management is a cornerstone of successful investing. This chapter, presented by Alex, explores comprehensive strategies and tools to mitigate investment risks while maximizing returns. Special attention is given to traditional risk management techniques, modern technologies, and the significant benefits of paper trading, which allows investors to practice strategies without risking actual capital.

Understanding Investment Risks

1. Types of Investment Risks:

Market Risk: Losses due to overall financial market performances.
Credit Risk: The possibility of a loss resulting from a borrower's failure to repay a loan or meet contractual obligations.
Liquidity Risk: The difficulty of quickly buying or selling investments without substantial price changes.
Operational Risk: Failures in internal processes, people, and systems, or from

The Millennial Investor: Simple Strategies for Long-Term Wealth.

external events.

2. AI in Risk Assessment:

Predictive Analysis: AI systems analyse large datasets to forecast market changes, helping investors anticipate potential downturns and adjust their strategies accordingly.
Portfolio Optimization: AI algorithms assist in diversifying investments to minimize risks associated with any single asset.

Proactive Risk Management Strategies

1. Diversification:

Asset Diversification: Spread investments across various asset types, such as stocks, bonds, and real estate, to mitigate risk.
Geographical Diversification: Investing in international markets can reduce exposure to the economic conditions of any one country.

2. Hedging:

Financial Instruments: Using options and futures to counterbalance potential losses in the markets.
Natural Hedges: Investing in counterbalancing assets to naturally offset risks, such as pairing investments in sectors that perform well during opposite economic cycles.

3. Implementing Stop-Loss Orders and Proper Position Sizing:

Stop-Loss Orders: Automatic orders that sell an asset when it reaches a certain price, limiting losses.

Position Sizing: Determining how much capital to allocate to different investments based on their risk level.

Enhancing Risk Management with Paper Trading

1. The Value of Paper Trading:

Risk-Free Practice: Paper trading, or virtual trading, allows investors to simulate trading strategies using fake money within real market conditions. This is crucial for beginners to gain experience without the financial risk.

Strategy Testing: Investors can test and refine their trading strategies and risk management practices using real-time data and market analysis without actual financial exposure.

2. Using Paper Trading Platforms:

Features and Tools: Many online platforms, such as Trading 212 and eToro, offer paper trading options that replicate live markets, providing users with a valuable learning experience.

Feedback and Improvement: These platforms often include analytical tools that help traders understand their trading behaviour and improve their decision-making processes.

Using Advanced Tools for Risk Management

1. Risk Management Software:

Simulation Tools: Software that can simulate various investment scenarios and their risk levels, helping investors make informed decisions.
AI Integration: Continuous data input improves AI's predictive capabilities, enhancing risk assessment models and recommendations.

2. Combining Expertise with Technology:

Robo-advisors and Human Advisors: Leveraging both AI-driven advice and human expertise can provide a balanced approach to risk management, blending personalized advice with efficient data processing.

Alex's Insights on Risk Management

From my perspective, the early stages of my investment journey were marked by several unexpected market shifts that taught me critical lessons about the importance of robust risk management. These experiences underscored the need to develop a resilient investing approach that could withstand market volatilities and still deliver the desired returns.

Integrating AI Tools with Traditional Methods
One of the most transformative steps in my investing strategy was the integration of AI tools with traditional investment methods. I began using AI to analyse large datasets, predict market trends, and identify potential investment opportunities that could have been easily overlooked. AI tools provided me with insights derived from complex patterns in market behaviour, which were beyond the reach of conventional analysis techniques. This allowed me to make more informed decisions, backed by data-driven

insights, which significantly enhanced the robustness of my investment strategies.

Practicing Strategies Through Paper Trading
Alongside integrating AI, I embraced paper trading as a vital part of my approach to managing investment risks. Paper trading enabled me to test out theories and strategies in a simulated environment without the risk of actual capital loss. This practice was instrumental in refining my investment tactics, allowing me to experiment with and adjust my portfolio in response to hypothetical market changes. It also helped me to fine-tune my risk management thresholds by providing a safe space to observe how different strategies performed under various market conditions.

Developing a Resilient Investing Approach
These strategies—leveraging AI for enhanced market insights and utilizing paper trading for risk-free strategy testing—culminated in a comprehensive and resilient approach to investing. This approach not only prepared me for potential risks but also equipped me to capitalize on opportunities swiftly and efficiently. It is a balanced method that carefully weighs potential risks against desired returns, ensuring that I remain aligned with my long-term financial goals while navigating the often-unpredictable market dynamics.

Reflecting on these experiences, I realize how crucial it is to continually adapt and enhance one's investment strategies. The integration of advanced technologies like AI with tried-and-true practices such as paper trading has not only fortified my investment portfolio but also instilled a greater confidence in my decision-making processes. For anyone looking to build a sustainable and robust investment strategy, I recommend embracing both technological advancements and traditional methods, as this combination has been instrumental in shaping a resilient approach to achieving desired financial outcomes.

Risk management in investing is essential for safeguarding assets and achieving long-term financial goals. By employing diversified strategies, leveraging advanced technologies, and practicing with paper trading, investors can enhance their ability to manage risks effectively and confidently pursue investment opportunities.

CHAPTER 15: BUILDING A PORTFOLIO

Creating a diversified investment portfolio is crucial for managing risk and achieving consistent returns over time. In this chapter, I, Alex, will guide you through the foundational strategies for building a robust investment portfolio. We'll explore the importance of diversification, how to allocate assets effectively, and the tools and techniques that can help you maintain a balanced portfolio tailored to your financial goals.

Understanding Portfolio Diversification
Diversification is the key to reducing risk in your investment portfolio. By spreading your investments across various asset classes, industries, and geographic regions, you can mitigate the impact of poor performance in any single area on your overall portfolio.

The Millennial Investor: Simple Strategies for Long-Term Wealth.

Concept of Diversification: Diversification involves investing in a variety of assets to reduce the volatility of your portfolio over time. This is because different asset classes often perform differently under the same economic conditions.

Benefits: A well-diversified portfolio can help you smooth out unsystematic risks and reduce the potential for large losses.

Asset Allocation

Asset allocation is the process of dividing an investment portfolio among different asset categories, such as stocks, bonds, real estate, and cash. This strategy is vital because it largely determines the risk and return characteristics of the portfolio.

Risk Tolerance and Time Horizon: Your asset allocation should be primarily influenced by your risk tolerance and investment time horizon. Younger investors might lean more towards stocks due to their potential for higher returns and longer recovery times, while those nearing retirement may prefer bonds for their stability and regular income.

Rebalancing: Regularly adjusting your portfolio to fit your asset allocation strategy is crucial. Market movements might cause your initial allocation percentages to shift, necessitating periodic rebalancing to maintain your risk level and strategy.

Implementing Diversification Strategies

To effectively diversify, you need to implement several strategies that encompass not just traditional investments like stocks and bonds but also alternative investments and new market opportunities.

Mix of Asset Types: Include a mix of different asset types. For instance, within equities, consider a variety of sectors such as technology, healthcare, and consumer goods. Within bonds, diversify between government and corporate bonds of different maturities and credit qualities.

Geographical Diversification: Investing in international markets can provide access to growth in different economies and additional diversification benefits.

Alternative Investments: Consider alternative assets such as real estate, commodities, or private equity, which often behave differently from standard stocks and bonds.

The Millennial Investor: Simple Strategies for Long-Term Wealth.

Tools for Building and Maintaining Your Portfolio
With the advent of technology, there are numerous tools available that can help investors build and maintain a diversified portfolio.

Investment Platforms: Platforms like E*TRADE, Charles Schwab, and Vanguard offer tools for portfolio construction and automatic rebalancing.
Robo-Advisors: Services like Betterment and Wealthfront use algorithms to manage your investments based on your risk tolerance and goals, adjusting your portfolio automatically to maintain diversification.

Alex's Personal Strategy
In my investing journey, I initially focused heavily on stocks but realized the importance of diversification during a market downturn. I began incorporating bonds and real estate into my portfolio, which helped stabilize my returns and reduce overall volatility. Over time, I have also explored more sophisticated strategies like using options for hedging and investing in international markets to capitalize on global growth opportunities.

Building a diversified investment portfolio is an ongoing process that requires understanding, strategy, and continual adjustment. By diversifying your investments, you can protect yourself against significant losses while positioning your portfolio for steady growth. Remember, the ultimate goal of investing is not just to maximize returns but to do so at a level of risk that is comfortable for you.

Section 4: Finding Your Side Hustle.

CHAPTER 16: IDENTIFYING PROFITABLE SIDE HUSTLES

In a dynamic economic landscape, cultivating multiple income streams can greatly enhance financial stability and independence. This chapter, led by Alex, explores the world of side hustles, providing practical guidance for identifying, starting, and growing a side business that aligns with your interests and lifestyle. We will also discuss how to leverage digital tools and platforms to maximize your side hustle success.

Identifying the Right-Side Hustle

1. Assess Your Skills and Interests:

Skill Inventory: List your skills, talents, and what you enjoy doing. Whether it is graphic design, writing, coding, or teaching, your side hustle should align with what you are good at and passionate about.

Market Demand: Research the current market to identify needs that match your skills. Tools like Google Trends or market research on platforms like Etsy and eBay can help you spot opportunities.

2. Feasibility and Resources:

Resource Evaluation: Consider what resources you already have or can easily acquire. This includes physical tools, online platforms, and even your network.
Time Management: Assess how much time you can realistically dedicate to a side hustle without compromising your primary responsibilities.
Setting Up Your Side Hustle

1. Business Planning:

Business Model: Define how you will generate income. Will you sell products, offer services, or use affiliate marketing? Outline your business structure, pricing strategy, and revenue model.

Legal Considerations: Register your business, if necessary, understand any licensing requirements, and consider consulting with a legal advisor to cover all bases.
2. Building an Online Presence:

Website and Social Media: Create a professional website and active social media profiles to promote your hustle. Platforms like WordPress for websites and Instagram or Facebook for social media marketing are invaluable tools.

E-commerce Platforms: If selling products, consider setting up shop on platforms like Shopify, Etsy, or Amazon to reach a broader audience.

Growing Your Side Hustle

1. Marketing and Promotion:

Digital Marketing: Utilize SEO, content marketing, and online advertising to draw attention to your services or products. Tools like Google AdWords and social media ads can be particularly effective.

Networking: Connect with other side hustlers and potential clients at events, through social media, and in online communities related to your hustle.

The Millennial Investor: Simple Strategies for Long-Term Wealth.

2. Scaling Your Operations:

Automation Tools: As your side hustle grows, use tools like Hootsuite for social media management or QuickBooks for accounting to save time and increase efficiency.

Outsourcing: Consider outsourcing tasks that are time-consuming or outside your skill set, such as web design or content creation, to focus on core activities.

Alex's Experience with Side Hustles

Drawing on my personal journey, I have learned firsthand how to transform a deep-rooted passion for photography into a lucrative side hustle. This endeavour not only supplemented my income but also fuelled my creative passion, showcasing the potential to turn personal interests into profitable ventures.

Developing the Business Concept
I started by identifying the dual opportunities within my passion for photography: selling my work and offering services at events. Recognizing the growing demand for unique, high-quality images and professional photography at events, I saw a chance to cater to both individuals seeking art and corporate or private clients needing event coverage.

Establishing an Online Presence
To reach a wider audience, I utilized several online platforms that serve as robust marketplaces for photographic work. I used sites like Shutterstock and Getty Images to sell my photos as stock images, creating a passive income stream that tapped into the global demand for diverse visual content. Additionally, I built a professional website to showcase my portfolio, which featured a variety of photography styles from landscape and lifestyle to portraits and event coverage.

On my website, I integrated e-commerce functionalities that allowed visitors to purchase prints and book photography sessions directly. This approach not only increased my sales but also allowed me to maintain control over my work and interactions with clients.

Engaging in Social Media and Digital Marketing
Knowing the impact of social media on brand building, I actively used platforms like Instagram, where visual content reigns supreme, to display my work. By posting new images regularly, engaging with followers in the comments, and utilizing targeted hashtags, I grew a significant online

following. This presence helped attract both photography enthusiasts and potential clients.

I also implemented digital marketing strategies, including SEO for my website to enhance searchability, and Google Ads to drive traffic to my online portfolio. Additionally, I sent out email marketing campaigns to my subscriber list with updates on new projects, special promotions on prints, and exclusive behind-the-scenes content to keep my audience engaged.

Offering Freelance Services at Local Events
To further expand my business, I tapped into the local market by offering professional photography services at events such as weddings, corporate gatherings, and community events. I networked with local businesses and event planners to get my name out there and demonstrate my ability to capture the essence of live events. My ability to produce vivid, engaging event photos led to referrals and repeat business, which solidified my reputation in the community.

Continuous Learning and Adaptation
I understood that staying relevant in the highly competitive photography industry required continuous learning and adaptation. I regularly updated my skills through online courses on advanced photography techniques and new technologies, such as drone photography and advanced photo editing software. This commitment to growth not only improved the quality of my work but also expanded my service offerings.

My experience from a photography enthusiast to a successful entrepreneur exemplifies how a side hustle can seamlessly combine personal passion with financial gain. By strategically leveraging online platforms, engaging in effective marketing, and continually evolving my skills, I built a sustainable business that not only supplements my income but also satisfies my creative aspirations. This journey underscores the viability of turning personal hobbies into profitable enterprises, provided there is a clear vision, strategic execution, and an unwavering passion for the craft.

Launching and growing a side hustle requires a clear understanding of your goals, strategic use of digital tools, and effective time management. By carefully planning and leveraging your skills, you can establish a fulfilling and profitable side business that enhances your financial security and personal satisfaction.

The Millennial Investor: Simple Strategies for Long-Term Wealth.

CHAPTER 17: E-COMMERCE AND ONLINE BUSINESSES

In this chapter, guided by Alex's experiences and strategic insights, we delve into the practical steps for launching four types of online businesses that require minimal startup capital. We will explore the potential revenue streams, necessary tools, and marketing strategies for each, helping you choose the best option to start your entrepreneurial journey.

1. Print on Demand

Business Overview:
Print on Demand (POD) allows you to sell your custom designs on various products such as t-shirts, mugs, and posters without holding inventory. This model uses third-party suppliers to handle everything from printing to shipping.

Tools and Platforms:
Platforms like Teespring, Printful, and Redbubble provide the infrastructure to create, sell, and distribute products adorned with your designs.

Potential Revenue:
Revenue varies based on product pricing and sales volume. For instance, selling a t-shirt for $25 with a production cost of £10 could net you £10 per sale. Successful sellers can generate between £500 to £10,000+ per month, depending on the niche and marketing efforts.

Marketing Strategies:
Utilize social media advertising, influencer partnerships, and SEO strategies to drive traffic to your product pages. Offering seasonal promotions and leveraging trends can also boost sales.

2. Affiliate Marketing

Business Overview:
Affiliate marketing involves promoting other companies' products and earning a commission for each sale made through your referral link.

Tools and Platforms:

Join affiliate programs through networks like Amazon Associates, Commission Junction, or ShareASale. You will receive a unique affiliate link to track your sales.

Potential Revenue:

Commissions range from 5% to 50% depending on the product category. Dedicated affiliate marketers can earn from a few hundred to several thousand dollars per month.

Marketing Strategies:

Create content-rich blogs or websites, utilize email marketing, and engage on social media platforms to promote your affiliate links. SEO optimization is crucial to drive organic traffic to your sites.

3. Dropshipping

Business Overview:
Dropshipping is a retail fulfilment method where you sell products on your website without managing inventory. When a customer makes a purchase, the order is sent to your supplier, who ships the products directly to the customer.

Tools and Platforms:
Platforms like Shopify and Oberlo support dropshipping by connecting you to suppliers and automating the sales process.

Potential Revenue:
Profit margins typically range from 10% to 30%. Successful dropshippers can earn thousands per month, but this varies widely based on niche competitiveness and marketing.

Marketing Strategies:
Leverage Facebook and Google Ads for quick traffic generation. Optimize your store for conversions and use retargeting strategies to increase sales.

4. Digital Products

Business Overview:
Selling digital products such as eBooks, courses, and software offers high-profit margins as you create the product once and sell it multiple times without additional costs.

Tools and Platforms:
Use platforms like Gumroad, Teachable, or Udemy to host and sell your

digital products.

Potential Revenue:
Revenues can vary significantly. For example, an eBook priced at £20 sold to five hundred people generates £10,000. Instructors on platforms like Udemy can earn anywhere from a few hundred to tens of thousands of dollars per month, depending on the popularity of their courses.

Marketing Strategies:
Content marketing, email newsletters, and webinars can be effective in promoting digital products. Paid advertising can also accelerate growth.

Alex's Insights on Starting a Print on Demand Business
When I decided to venture into the online business world, I chose a print on demand (POD) model focusing on custom-designed apparel for fitness enthusiasts. This chapter shares the comprehensive journey of establishing that venture, highlighting the integration of passion with business, and emphasizing the importance of adaptability, resilience, and ongoing learning.

Choosing the Niche
Selecting the right niche was the first crucial step in my entrepreneurial journey. I was passionate about fitness and noticed a gap in the market for motivational fitness apparel. This niche not only tapped into a growing trend of personalized workout gear but also connected with a community that valued health and motivation. This decision shaped all aspects of my business strategy, from product design to marketing and customer engagement.

Building the Business
Setting Up the Platform:
I used Shopify, a user-friendly e-commerce platform that seamlessly integrates with various POD services. Shopify's robust infrastructure allowed me to focus on creating designs and marketing my products without worrying about the technicalities of website management.

Choosing the Right POD Partner:
I partnered with Printful for their reliability and quality of products. Printful's integration with Shopify meant that once a customer placed an order, Printful would manage the printing, packaging, and shipping. This setup minimized my upfront costs and eliminated the need for inventory storage.

Design Tools:
For designing the apparel, I utilized tools like Adobe Illustrator and Canva. These tools helped in crafting high-quality, unique designs that resonated with my target audience. I focused on creating motivational quotes and graphics

that appealed to fitness enthusiasts looking for ways to express their dedication through their attire.

Marketing the Business
Social Media Engagement:
Platforms like Instagram and Facebook were instrumental in building and engaging with my community. By sharing customer testimonials, posting interactive content, and highlighting new designs, I established a strong online presence that drove both sales and brand loyalty.

Content Marketing:
I maintained a blog on my website where I shared fitness tips, success stories from customers, and behind-the-scenes looks at the design process. This content not only boosted SEO but also added value for my customers, making my brand a part of their fitness journey.

Email Marketing:
I used email marketing to keep my customers informed about new product launches and exclusive promotions. Tools like Mailchimp allowed me to automate my email campaigns and segment my audience for more personalized messaging.

Scaling the Business
As demand increased, scaling the business required more than just managing larger order volumes. It involved refining the product range, introducing new categories beyond apparel such as accessories and home decor, and expanding the reach to international markets.

Customer Feedback:
Listening to customer feedback was crucial during the scaling process. It helped me understand what designs were most popular and what new products customers wanted to see.

Adaptation and Innovation:
The fitness industry is fast-evolving and staying relevant meant continuously innovating and adapting my product offerings based on the latest fitness trends and customer preferences.

Starting and running a print on demand business taught me the importance of meshing personal passions with professional pursuits. It highlighted the need for flexibility, continuous market research, and leveraging the right tools to streamline operations. Most importantly, it underscored the value of resilience and adaptability in the ever-changing landscape of online entrepreneurship.

The Millennial Investor: Simple Strategies for Long-Term Wealth.

Starting an online business with minimal capital is highly feasible and can be lucrative. By selecting the right model, leveraging efficient online platforms, and implementing strategic marketing, aspiring entrepreneurs can launch a cost-effective business with substantial growth potential.

CHAPTER 18: FREELANCING

Freelancing offers a flexible and scalable way to monetize your skills directly from your home or anywhere in the world. In this chapter, guided by Alex's expertise and experiences, we will explore how to turn your professional abilities into a thriving freelance business. We will discuss how to identify marketable skills, establish your online presence, and effectively manage client relationships to build a sustainable freelancing career.

Identifying Marketable Skills

1. Skill Assessment:

The Millennial Investor: Simple Strategies for Long-Term Wealth.

Overview: Identify skills that have high demand in the freelance market such as web development, graphic design, content writing, or specialized consultancy in areas such as marketing or finance.
Tools for Assessment: Use platforms like LinkedIn and Glassdoor to research which skills are in demand and what clients are looking for in freelancers.

2. Continuous Skill Improvement:

Importance of Upgrading: To stay competitive, continually enhance your skills through online courses and certifications.
Platforms for Learning: Websites like Coursera, Udemy, and LinkedIn Learning offer a wide range of courses that can help you stay relevant in your field.
Setting Up Your Freelancing Business

1. Building Your Portfolio:

Purpose: Showcase your best work to attract clients by highlighting your expertise and successful projects.
Tools: Create a professional portfolio using website builders like Wix or WordPress or utilize portfolio platforms like Behance or Dribbble.

2. Establishing Online Presence:

Creating a Professional Website: Use platforms like Squarespace or WordPress to build a website that includes your portfolio, services, and contact information.
Utilizing Freelance Marketplaces: Register on sites like Upwork, Freelancer, and Fiverr to gain access to a global client base.
3. Legal and Financial Setup:

Business Registration: Depending on your location, you may need to register as a sole proprietorship or form an LLC.
Financial Management: Set up a system for tracking your earnings and expenses, considering tools like QuickBooks or FreshBooks.
Finding Clients and Managing Projects

1. Marketing Your Services:

Networking: Attend industry conferences, join professional groups on LinkedIn, and participate in online forums related to your skills.
Social Media Marketing: Leverage social media platforms to share your work, engage with potential clients, and establish your brand.

The Millennial Investor: Simple Strategies for Long-Term Wealth.

2. Client Proposals and Negotiations:

Crafting Proposals: Develop tailored proposals that clearly outline the scope of work, pricing, and deliverables.
Negotiation Skills: Learn to negotiate contracts that are fair and beneficial for both parties.

3. Project and Client Management:

Communication: Maintain clear and regular communication with clients to manage expectations and project timelines.
Feedback: Actively seek client feedback to improve your services and customer satisfaction.

Scaling Your Freelance Business
1. Outsourcing and Delegation:

Hiring Help: As your business grows, consider outsourcing tasks such as accounting, marketing, or even certain client projects to other freelancers.
Delegation Tools: Use project management tools like Asana or Trello to keep track of delegated tasks and project progress.
2. Building Long-Term Client Relationships:

Retention Strategies: Offer excellent service, follow-up regularly, and consider offering incentives for repeat business or referrals.
Growth Through Reputation: Focus on building a strong reputation through consistent quality work and professional integrity.
Alex's Insights on Freelancing: Leveraging Fiverr for Consulting in Print on Demand
My journey through the world of freelancing has been diverse and enriching, starting as a freelance graphic designer and evolving into establishing a full-service digital marketing agency. One of the pivotal aspects of my freelancing career was using Fiverr to offer consulting services, helping others start their own print on demand websites. This experience not only expanded my skills but also deepened my understanding of the digital marketplace and entrepreneurship.

Starting Out on Fiverr
I initially joined Fiverr as a way to supplement my income while pursuing my passion for graphic design. However, I soon realized the platform's potential for broader business opportunities. My experience in designing and managing my own print on demand business had given me valuable insights and skills that were in high demand. Seeing this, I decided to offer consulting services

specifically tailored to helping others launch and optimize their print on demand ventures.

Developing a Niche Consulting Service
Fiverr allowed me to niche down my offerings. I focused specifically on clients who wanted to enter the print on demand industry but lacked the technical knowledge or marketing expertise to get started. My services ranged from providing initial setup advice, including choosing the right platforms and products, to more advanced marketing strategies to enhance online visibility and sales.

1. Tailored Advice:

Platform Selection: Guiding clients on choosing platforms that best fit their business model, whether they were looking to integrate with Shopify, WooCommerce, or use standalone platforms like Teespring.
Product Selection: Advising on product selections that align with current market trends and their target audience's preferences.
2. Marketing Strategies:

Brand Development: Helping clients establish a cohesive brand identity that resonates with their target market.
Digital Marketing Tactics: Implementing SEO strategies, social media marketing, and content creation to drive traffic and sales.
Challenges and Rewards
Challenges:

One of the major challenges was ensuring that clients with varying levels of technical skills could understand and implement the strategies I advised. This required me to develop clear, easy-to-follow guides and tutorials.
Managing client expectations was another challenge, especially when dealing with clients new to online entrepreneurship who expected quick results.
Rewards:

The most rewarding aspect was seeing my clients succeed and knowing that I had played a part in their entrepreneurial journey. Many of my clients were able to turn their small projects into profitable businesses, which in turn led to more referrals and a solid reputation on Fiverr.
This experience also enhanced my own skills in digital marketing and e-commerce, contributing significantly to my professional growth and the eventual expansion into my own full-service agency.
Leveraging Success into Agency Growth
The success and reputation I built on Fiverr provided the foundation to expand my freelancing into a full-service digital marketing agency. The

network I built, the client testimonials I gathered, and the vast experience I gained from various projects were instrumental in this transition.

My experience on Fiverr as a consultant for print on demand businesses has been a cornerstone of my freelancing career. It taught me the importance of adaptability, the value of continuous learning, and the effectiveness of building a strong professional network. These elements are crucial not just in freelancing but in any business endeavor, and they continue to influence how I run my agency today.

Freelancing is a powerful way to build a career on your own terms, using skills you are passionate about. By effectively marketing your services, managing projects efficiently, and maintaining robust client relationships, you can turn freelancing from a side hustle into a main source of income.

CHAPTER 19: REAL ESTATE AND PASSIVE INCOME

Investing in rental properties has been a significant part of my financial strategy, offering a consistent source of income and the potential for capital appreciation. Here, I will share my journey and insights into entering the rental property market, highlighting the importance of strategic planning, understanding market dynamics, and maintaining properties to optimize investment returns.

Understanding the Rental Property Market
My first step into the rental property market involved a deep dive into market research. I needed to understand which geographic areas offered the best potential for rental yields and capital appreciation. Factors like local economic stability, population growth, and future development plans were critical in my decision-making process.

Market Research:

Location Analysis: I focused on areas with high rental demand, such as those near universities, business districts, or major transportation hubs.
Economic Indicators: Assessing the local job market, average income levels, and economic trends helped me predict the long-term viability of my investments.
Selecting the Right Property
Choosing the right property required balancing cost considerations with potential returns. I looked for properties that offered the best value for money, which often meant purchasing units that needed some level of renovation to enhance their value.

Property Selection Criteria:

Condition and Potential for Improvement: Properties that required cosmetic updates tended to offer better deals; they cost less upfront and provided an opportunity to add value.
Tenant Appeal: I chose properties with features most desired by renters, such as good natural light, ample parking, and proximity to amenities like shops and public transport.
Financial Aspects of Rental Investments
Financing the purchase of rental properties was another area where careful planning was essential. I explored various financing options to find the most cost-effective and flexible solutions.

Financing Options:

Mortgages: Securing a competitive interest rate was crucial. I shopped around for the best mortgage deals that offered flexibility in terms of overpayments and refinancing options.

Leveraging Equity: In some cases, I used the equity from existing properties to finance additional purchases, thereby expanding my portfolio without the need for external financing.

Managing Rental Properties

Effective property management has been key to maintaining the profitability of my rental investments. This includes everything from tenant selection to ongoing property maintenance.

Tenant Management:

Screening Process: I developed a thorough screening process to ensure that I selected reliable tenants who would pay rent on time and maintain the property well.

Lease Agreements: Clear and comprehensive lease agreements helped set the right expectations and provided legal protection for both parties.

Property Maintenance:

Regular Inspections: Regular inspections and maintenance helped preserve the value of the property and prevent minor issues from developing into major expenses.

Professional Management: As my portfolio grew, I hired a property management company to handle day-to-day management, which allowed me to focus on strategic growth and other business interests.

Scaling Your Rental Investments

Scaling my investment in rental properties involved not only acquiring more properties but also diversifying into diverse types of real estate, such as commercial properties and multi-family units. This diversification helped spread risk and increased the potential for higher returns.

Alex's Continued Journey in Real Estate Investment

Following the successful flip of my first property—a small flat in the UK—I found myself at a pivotal moment in my real estate investment journey. The profit I earned from that initial flip not only boosted my confidence but also provided the capital necessary to expand my portfolio. Here, I will share how I leveraged that success to purchase another property to flip and a second property to rent out, applying the strategic insights and practices I had honed from my first experience.

The Millennial Investor: Simple Strategies for Long-Term Wealth.

Leveraging Profits for Further Investments

The success of my first flip was exhilarating; it was a clear demonstration of the potential in real estate investment. With the profit from that sale, I decided to reinvest in the market, purchasing a second property to flip and another to hold as a rental. This dual approach allowed me to capitalize on quick gains while building a steady income stream.

1. Buying Another Flip Property:

Market Research: Using the insights gained from my first flip, I spent considerable time researching the market to find another property with enormous potential. I targeted an emerging neighborhood known for its development plans and increasing property values.

Value-Add Potential: The property I chose needed more significant renovations than my first project. However, armed with more experience and a better network of contractors, I was prepared for the challenge. I focused on making impactful updates that would appeal broadly to buyers, such as modernizing the kitchen and bathrooms and improving the home's energy efficiency.

2. Acquiring a Rental Property:

Location Selection: For my rental property, I chose a location near a major university and several business parks, ensuring consistent demand from students and young professionals.

Property Features: I selected a property that required minimal updates to keep initial costs low. It also featured desirable amenities like in-unit laundry and private parking, which were significant draws for potential tenants.
Financial Strategies and Property Management

Financing the Purchases:

Leveraging Equity: Using the equity from my first flip, I secured mortgages for both new properties at competitive rates. This strategy not only helped me conserve cash but also spread my financial risk across multiple investments.
Cost Management: I was meticulous about budgeting for renovations and set aside a contingency fund to manage unexpected expenses, a lesson learned from my first flipping experience.

Managing the Rental Property:

Tenant Screening: I implemented a rigorous screening process to ensure I found reliable tenants, minimizing the risk of rental arrears and property damage.

Maintenance Planning: I established a proactive maintenance schedule for the rental property to ensure it remained in excellent condition, enhancing tenant satisfaction and retaining value.

Scaling and Diversification

With two more properties under my management, I began to see the real potential of real estate not just as a series of transactions, but as a long-term investment strategy. This experience reinforced the importance of diversification—not just across different stocks or bonds, but within real estate itself, balancing flips with long-term rental holdings.

Reflections and Future Directions

The journey from my first property flip to managing multiple real estate investments taught me invaluable lessons about the importance of strategic planning, market research, and economic management. It has set a foundation for my ongoing investment strategy, where I continue to balance high-return flips with the stable income of rental properties. Looking ahead, I plan to further diversify my real estate portfolio, possibly venturing into commercial properties to capitalize on new market opportunities.

This progression in my real estate investment journey underscores the power of leveraging initial successes to fuel further growth. By smartly reinvesting profits and applying lessons learned from each project, I have not only expanded my portfolio but also solidified my approach to achieving sustained success in the real estate market.

Investing in rental properties has been both challenging and rewarding. It requires a well-thought-out strategy, in-depth market knowledge, and effective property management. However, the financial rewards and the stability of income it provides have made it a worthwhile endeavor. Through careful planning and management, rental property investment can be a powerful tool for building wealth and achieving long-term financial goals.

CHAPTER 20: TURNING HOBBIES INTO INCOME:

In the realm of entrepreneurship, the journey from a side hustle to a significant business success is both inspiring and instructive. This chapter delves into the real-world stories of three young entrepreneurs who transformed their modest beginnings into prominent business ventures. These narratives not only shed light on the pathways to success but also underscore the combination of innovation, perseverance, and strategic thinking required to scale a business in today's competitive environment.

The Millennial Investor: Simple Strategies for Long-Term Wealth.

Astrid & Miyu - From Online Beginnings to Physical Retail Success Beginnings:

Astrid & Miyu was founded by Connie Nam in 2012. Inspired by her travels and experiences in markets around the world during her youth, Nam wanted to create a jewellery brand that captured the emotional and sentimental value she felt during those times. With just £500, she launched a website and used her social media savvy to quickly gain visibility, acquiring 20,000 followers in the first year (ScaleUp Institute).

Growth and Expansion:
Astrid & Miyu initially focused on online sales but always had an eye on physical retail. The brand tested the waters with pop-up stores before opening its first permanent store in 2015, funded by angel investors. This move was pivotal, proving the value of an integrated online-offline retail approach. The brand saw significant growth post-lockdown as it capitalized on favorable retail leases, further expanding its physical presence.

Challenges:
Despite its success, Astrid & Miyu faced challenges typical of the jewellery market, including securing funding from investors who did not initially understand the brand's potential. The brand also navigated the impacts of the COVID-19 pandemic, which forced a temporary shift back towards online sales as foot traffic decreased.

Financial Performance:
By 2021, Astrid & Miyu had graced prestigious league tables such as The Sunday Times Fast Track and JP Morgan's Top 200 Female Powered Businesses. The company was balancing revenue between e-commerce and retail, aiming for a 50-50 split. In 2023, the brand projected significant revenues of £35 million, highlighting its successful scale-up

Future Outlook:
Astrid & Miyu is focusing on international expansion, with particular emphasis on the US and European markets. The brand aims to balance the growth of its physical stores with its strong online presence, continuing to innovate in both spaces.

Astrid & Miyu's journey from a simple idea inspired by market travels to a multimillion-pound business exemplifies the power of strategic growth, effective use of social media, and the ability to adapt to market changes. The brand continues to evolve, driven by a sharp vision and a strong understanding of its consumer base. *Ref (BDO UK) (ScaleUp Institute).

The Millennial Investor: Simple Strategies for Long-Term Wealth.

The Adir Group – Pioneering Property Development

Gal and Tania Adir are young entrepreneurs who have carved out a successful niche in the UK property market. Beginning their careers in finance and law, they soon transitioned to property development, founding G&T London at the young ages of 23 and 24. Their focus on high value, centrally located flats and innovative projects like Nuper has distinguished them in a competitive industry.

Founding and Initial Projects

The Adirs' journey in property development began after they left their corporate jobs, driven by a desire to create something entrepreneurial. They established G&T London and initially focused on renovating single high-value flats. Their early projects were marked by meticulous attention to detail and a keen sense of the market's demand, which quickly led to significant achievements.

Breakthrough Project

One of their most notable early successes was the refurbishment of a Georgian building at 58 Myddelton Square. The project was a turning point, selling for over £5 million and setting a record for the most expensive single house ever sold in Islington at that time. This success solidified their reputation and provided the capital and confidence to pursue even larger and more ambitious projects.

Transition to the Adir Group and Nuper

As their success grew, Gal and Tania evolved their business into the Adir Group, expanding their scope to include more complex development projects. One of the innovative concepts they introduced was Nuper, a co-operative live-work scheme aimed at a younger demographic. This project reflects their vision to adapt to the changing needs of urban dwellers and addresses the affordability crisis in major cities like London.

Financial Growth and Current Status

The Adir Group has continued to expand its portfolio, with reported developments valued at approximately £50 million. Their projects typically focus on sustainability and community-enhancing features, appealing to socially conscious investors and residents alike. The Nuper project, in particular, showcases their commitment to providing value beyond mere housing—offering community and a shared living-working environment that resonates with modern urbanites.

Gal and Tania Adir's transition from corporate professionals to pioneering property developers exemplifies the dynamic potential of the real estate sector. Their ability to identify and capitalize on niche markets, combined with a bold approach to development, has not only yielded substantial financial success but also contributed positively to the urban landscape. Their journey from renovating flats to developing innovative living solutions like Nuper underscores the evolution of property development to meet contemporary needs and challenges.

The Adir Group stands as a testament to the impact that visionary entrepreneurs can have in transforming the property market through innovative concepts and strong market insights.

Ben Francis and Gymshark

Ben Francis founded Gymshark in 2012 at the age of nineteen while still a university student and a part-time pizza delivery man. What began as a screen-printing operation in a garage has since blossomed into a globally recognized fitness apparel and accessories brand, valued at over £1 billion. This case study explores the rise of Gymshark from a small start-up to a leading player in the global fitness apparel industry.

Early Days and Concept
Ben Francis started Gymshark with a group of high-school friends, combining their passion for fitness and expertise in technology. Initially, the company focused on producing fitness apparel that Francis and his team would want to wear themselves, which at the time was not available in the market. They began by screen-printing designs onto gym vests and t-shirts, selling them directly from the Gymshark website.

Growth and Innovation
The turning point for Gymshark came when they began to utilize the burgeoning power of social media and influencer marketing. Francis recognized the potential of sponsorship and partnerships with fitness influencers on platforms like YouTube and Instagram, which were rapidly growing in popularity. By sending out apparel to influencers for review and exposure, Gymshark tapped into a vast audience of fitness enthusiasts.

Expansion and Challenges
As the brand grew, Gymshark faced several challenges, particularly with supply chain and distribution. The demand often outstripped supply, leading to sold-out products and website crashes, notably during major sales events. To address these issues, Francis made significant investments in logistics and IT infrastructure, moving production from the UK to overseas to scale up manufacturing and streamline operations.

Business Model and Strategy
Gymshark's direct-to-consumer business model bypasses traditional retail, allowing for greater control over the brand and customer experience. This model also enables Gymshark to maintain higher profit margins and agility in product development. Gymshark's focus on community building through events like pop-up shops and fitness meets has solidified a strong brand community.

Current Status and Future Outlook
Today, Gymshark has customers in 180 countries and has continued to grow with offices in the UK, Hong Kong, and the USA. The company was valued at over £1 billion in 2020, following a minority investment from General Atlantic, catapulting it into the ranks of "unicorn" startups. Ben Francis returned as CEO in 2021 to steer the company through its next phase of growth, focusing on sustainability and expanding into new markets.

Ben Francis's journey with Gymshark is a quintessential example of entrepreneurial success in the digital age. From humble beginnings in a garage to a billion-pound enterprise, Gymshark exemplifies how innovative business models, coupled with a keen understanding of digital marketing and community engagement, can lead to extraordinary growth. The future looks promising for Gymshark as it continues to innovate and expand its global presence in the fitness apparel industry.

The journeys of Ben Francis with Gymshark, Gal and Tania Adir with the Adir Group, and Connie Nam with Astrid & Miyu exemplify the potential for remarkable success when innovative ideas meet niche market needs. Each of these entrepreneurs started with a clear vision and a deep understanding of their respective markets—whether it be fitness apparel, property development, or jewellery. Their stories underscore the critical importance of adapting to market demands and leveraging digital platforms to enhance brand visibility and engagement. These case studies not only highlight the power of strategic thinking and resilience but also serve as a blueprint for aspiring entrepreneurs on how to effectively combine passion with business acumen to build and scale successful enterprises in today's dynamic and competitive environment.

The Millennial Investor: Simple Strategies for Long-Term Wealth.

Section 5:

Investing in yourself.

CHAPTER 21: THE WINNING MENTALITY: DEVELOPING THE MINDSET FOR SUCCESS

Success, indeed, begins in the mind. In this chapter, we delve deep into the psychological foundations that support high achievers across various fields, illustrating how resilience, optimism, effective goal setting, and a proactive approach to challenges are essential traits that can dramatically enhance your capacity to realize your ambitions. Here, we explore practical tips and strategies designed to cultivate a winning mentality, empowering you to navigate obstacles and capitalize on opportunities with enhanced confidence and determination.

Understanding the Winning Mentality
A winning mentality is not an inherent trait possessed from birth; rather, it is cultivated through consistent practice and mindset conditioning. This mentality involves a combination of mental resilience, a positive outlook, strategic planning, and proactive behavior. By fostering these characteristics, individuals can create a robust mental framework that propels them towards their goals.

Cultivating Resilience
Resilience is the backbone of a winning mentality. It is the ability to bounce back from setbacks, learn from failure, and continue to move forward with an even stronger resolve.

Practical Exercise: Start by setting small, manageable goals that challenge your current capabilities. As you face obstacles and push through discomfort, your resilience will naturally build.
Real-Life Application: Reflect on past failures and reframe them as learning opportunities. Analyze what went wrong, what you learned, and how you can adjust your strategies moving forward.
Fostering Optimism
Optimism in this context does not mean being blindly positive but rather maintaining a constructive outlook that focuses on finding solutions rather than dwelling on problems. Optimistic individuals tend to approach barriers with a can-do attitude, which significantly increases the likelihood of success.

Technique for Development: Practice gratitude daily. By acknowledging and appreciating what you have, you can shift your mindset from one of scarcity to one of abundance, which is conducive to optimism.
Example: Each morning, write down three things for which you are grateful. This simple exercise can transform your outlook and open your mind to

possibilities.

Effective Goal Setting

Clear and precise goal setting is critical. Well-defined goals provide direction and a benchmark for success. They act as a roadmap, guiding your actions and providing motivation.

Strategy Session: Utilize the SMART goal framework — Specific, Measurable, Achievable, Relevant, Time-bound. This structure ensures that your goals are well-crafted and conducive to real progress.

Implementation: Break each goal into actionable steps. For instance, if your goal is to start a business, begin by researching the market, then move on to writing a business plan, followed by securing funding.

Proactive Approach to Challenges

A proactive approach involves anticipating potential challenges and preparing for them in advance, rather than reacting to problems as they arise.

Action Plan: Regularly assess potential risks in your personal and professional life. Develop contingency plans for those scenarios.

Practical Example: If you are aiming for a promotion, identify skills that you need to improve or acquire. Start working on those skills before it is time for your performance review.

Alex's Insights: Cultivating a Winning Mentality

Throughout my journey, both personal and professional, the importance of developing a winning mentality has been a consistent theme. When I first embarked on my entrepreneurial path, I quickly realized that mindset was just as critical as skillset. This understanding came from observing not only my successes but also how I handled failures and setbacks.

The Early Days

In the early days of my career, I faced numerous challenges that tested my resolve and determination. There were moments when things did not go as planned projects fell through, clients backed out, and financial targets were not met. It was during these times that the real power of a positive and resilient mindset became evident. Instead of succumbing to discouragement, I chose to view each setback as a stepping stone to greater success.

Building Resilience

Resilience did not come naturally to me; it was a skill I consciously developed over time. I remember setting small, challenging goals for myself, pushing the boundaries of what I thought was possible. Each minor victory built my confidence, and each failure taught me valuable lessons. This cycle of setting goals, facing challenges, and learning from the outcomes became the backbone of my growth strategy.

The Millennial Investor: Simple Strategies for Long-Term Wealth.

Maintaining Optimism
Optimism has been a key driver in maintaining my momentum. I made it a practice to start each day by listing three things for which I was grateful. This simple habit helped shift my focus from the problems at hand to the opportunities that lay ahead. It reminded me that no matter the current difficulties, there was always a reason to remain hopeful and driven.

Strategic Goal Setting
Goal setting was another critical element. Early in my career, I learned the importance of setting SMART goals—specific, measurable, achievable, relevant, and time-bound. This approach forced me to think critically about my ambitions, break them down into actionable steps, and regularly review my progress. It was not just about setting goals but setting the right goals that aligned with my long-term vision.

A Proactive Approach
Adopting a proactive approach to challenges meant anticipating potential issues and planning accordingly. I learned to regularly analyse my projects and identify areas where things could go wrong. This foresight allowed me to develop contingency plans and react swiftly when needed, minimizing the impact of any disruptions.

Reflecting on the Journey
Looking back, I see that developing a winning mentality was not a single event but a continuous process. It required consistent effort, a willingness to adapt, and a commitment to personal growth. The mindset strategies I cultivated have not only propelled me towards my professional goals but have also enhanced my personal life, allowing me to enjoy a fulfilling and balanced existence.

Conclusion
In sharing these insights, my hope is to inspire others to recognize the profound impact a winning mentality can have on their lives. It is about more than just facing the day-to-day challenges; it is about transforming the way you think, which in turn, transforms the way you live and succeed. Embrace the journey of building a strong mindset, for it is the most reliable predictor of achieving and surpassing your goals.

Developing a winning mentality is a dynamic and ongoing process. It requires diligence, self-reflection, and an unwavering commitment to personal growth. By embracing resilience, optimism, strategic goal setting, and a proactive attitude, you equip yourself with the tools necessary to overcome any obstacle and seize every opportunity. This chapter not only lays the foundation for building a mindset geared towards success but also empowers you to

The Millennial Investor: Simple Strategies for Long-Term Wealth.

transform your aspirations into achievable realities.

CHAPTER 22: LIFELONG LEARNING: IMPORTANCE OF CONTINUOUS EDUCATION AND WHERE TO FOCUS

In an ever-evolving world, the commitment to lifelong learning stands as a pivotal element in sustaining personal growth and professional success. As your guide, I, Alex, will delve into the significance of ongoing education, outline areas where focusing your learning efforts can yield the greatest dividends, and offer practical advice for integrating continuous learning into your daily life.

The Power of Continuous Learning

Lifelong learning goes beyond formal education; it encompasses a broad spectrum of activities including reading, attending workshops, engaging in professional development courses, and more. This chapter underscores how staying intellectually active and continuously acquiring new knowledge not only enhances your skills but also keeps you adaptable in the face of changing industries and global landscapes.

Identifying Key Learning Areas

1. Industry-Specific Skills:

Overview: Keep abreast of the latest technologies, techniques, and theories in your field. Whether you are in technology, finance, healthcare, or any other sector, understanding emerging trends can position you as a leader rather than a follower.
Tools for Learning: Use industry-specific publications, join professional associations, and participate in specialized training sessions.

2. Interdisciplinary Skills:

Significance: Skills such as critical thinking, problem-solving, communication, and leadership are universally valued and can dramatically enhance your ability

to work across various contexts.
Development Strategies: Engage in diverse experiences, such as cross-functional projects or learning courses on platforms like Coursera or Udemy that focus on these core competencies.

Leveraging Modern Learning Tools
In today's digital age, there are myriad resources available to facilitate ongoing education. Emphasizing self-directed learning through digital platforms allows for a tailored educational experience that can fit into even the busiest schedules.

Online Platforms: Websites like Coursera, Udemy, and Khan Academy offer courses on a vast array of subjects, often free or at a low cost. These platforms provide flexibility to learn at your own pace and on your own schedule.
Mobile Learning: Apps on smartphones and tablets enable learning to on-the-go. Podcasts, audiobooks, and app-based courses mean your commute or gym time can also become a learning session.

Building a Routine for Lifelong Learning

1. Daily Learning Goals:

Implementing Small Daily Objectives: Set manageable learning goals each day. It could be as simple as reading an article, watching a tutorial video, or completing a single lesson in an online course.
Example: Dedicate 30 minutes each morning to reading industry-related news or insights from thought leaders on LinkedIn.

2. Integrative Learning Practices:

Application: Apply what you learn by undertaking projects or tasks that utilize new skills or knowledge. This could mean proposing a new project at work or starting a personal endeavor that allows you to use new tools and techniques.
Reflective Practice: Keep a journal of your learning experiences and reflect on how each session can be applied to improve your professional or personal life.

Alex's Insights: Leveraging Online Learning for Investment Success
When I first contemplated diving into the world of investing, I knew I was stepping into unfamiliar territory. The financial markets are vast and can be incredibly complex, and I was acutely aware of the steep learning curve ahead of me. My goal was not just to participate but to excel and make informed,

strategic investment decisions. This led me to explore various educational resources, and that is when I discovered the immense value of online learning platforms, particularly Udemy.

Embracing Online Learning
Udemy became a pivotal resource in my educational journey. I was drawn to its diverse range of courses, especially those focused on investment strategies and market analysis. The course that caught my attention was titled "Investment Strategies for Beginners," and it promised a comprehensive overview of the basics, along with insights into advanced techniques.

Course Structure: The course was structured into manageable modules, each focusing on various aspects of investing, from the fundamentals of the stock market to more intricate strategies like options trading and commodities investments. This modular approach allowed me to pace my learning according to my daily schedule without feeling overwhelmed.

Practical Application: What made the course especially impactful was its emphasis on real-world application. It was not just theoretical knowledge; each module included practical examples and even simulated investment scenarios. This hands-on approach was instrumental in solidifying my understanding and boosting my confidence.

Applying New Knowledge
Equipped with new strategies and a deeper understanding of the investment landscape, I felt prepared to begin my investment journey. I started small, applying the principles I learned to make initial investments in low-risk stocks and bonds. As my confidence grew, so did my portfolio. I ventured into more volatile markets, armed with strategies that I had practiced during my coursework.

Continuous Learning: The initial success of my investments encouraged me to delve deeper. I returned to Udemy and enrolled in more advanced courses, each time focusing on various aspects of investing. This continuous cycle of learning and applying helped me not only expand my portfolio but also minimize risks and maximize returns.

Reflections on the Impact of Online Learning
Looking back, I attribute a significant part of my investment success to the solid educational foundation I built through online courses. Udemy and similar platforms provided me with the flexibility to learn at my own pace and the depth of knowledge necessary to navigate the complexities of various markets.

Advice to Aspiring Investors: For anyone looking to start their investment journey, I cannot overstate the importance of education. Invest in your learning as diligently as you would in the financial markets. Choose courses that offer both theoretical knowledge and practical application, and never stop learning. The financial world evolves, and so should your strategies.

Conclusion

The decision to use Udemy for learning investment strategies was a turning point in my life. It transformed me from a novice to a knowledgeable investor, equipped to make decisions that have yielded substantial returns. My journey underscores the importance of lifelong learning and the role of accessible education in personal and professional growth.

Lifelong learning is more than an academic endeavor—it is a way of life that can enrich your firsthand experiences and enhance your professional capabilities. By fostering a curiosity for new knowledge and understanding the value of continuous education, you equip yourself with the tools to succeed no matter the changes that come your way. Remember, the investment you make in your education is the most rewarding investment you can make, yielding dividends in all aspects of life.

.

CHAPTER 23: HEALTH AND WEALTH: HOW GOOD HEALTH SUPPORTS FINANCIAL SUCCESS

In the pursuit of financial goals, it is essential not to overlook one of your most valuable assets: your health. In this chapter, I, Alex, will explore the profound impact that maintaining good health has on personal effectiveness and financial stability. We will discuss practical ways to prioritize health in daily life and how this foundation supports and enhances your ability to achieve and enjoy your success.

The Connection Between Health and Financial Success

Health directly influences your capacity to perform, achieve, and enjoy the fruits of your labour. It is not just about avoiding illness; it is about optimizing your physical and mental well-being to enhance all aspects of life, including financial success.

Increased Productivity: Being in good health means fewer sick days, higher energy levels, and greater mental clarity—all of which lead to increased productivity and better performance at work.

Long-term Cost Savings: Preventative health care, regular exercise, and a balanced diet can significantly decrease the likelihood of chronic diseases, which are not only costly but can also lead to prolonged income disruption.

Mental Sharpness: A healthy lifestyle supports robust mental health, critical for making sound decisions, particularly in high-stakes environments like investments and business management.

Key Components of a Healthy Lifestyle

Achieving and maintaining good health involves several key components, each contributing to overall well-being and, consequently, financial success.

Balanced Diet: Nutrition plays a crucial role in maintaining energy and preventing diseases. A diet rich in fruits, vegetables, lean proteins, and whole grains provides the nutrients necessary for optimal body function.

Regular Exercise: Physical activity is not only good for the body but also for the mind. It improves mood, reduces stress, and enhances cognitive functions, making it easier to tackle complex tasks and manage stress.

Adequate Sleep: Quality sleep is crucial for physical repair and cognitive function. Consistently good sleep helps maintain focus, improves decision-making, and manages emotional and psychological stress.
Stress Management: Managing stress through techniques such as meditation, yoga, and regular relaxation can prevent burnout and maintain overall mental health.

Practical Steps to Prioritize Health
Integrating health-conscious habits into your daily routine does not have to be daunting. Here are practical steps to make health a priority:

Health Education: Stay informed about health and wellness to make educated decisions about diet, exercise, and lifestyle.

Work-Life Balance: It is crucial to manage your professional responsibilities without compromising your health. Ensure you have time for relaxation and hobbies that relieve stress.

Integrating Health into Daily Life

Creating Healthy Habits: Small, sustainable changes can lead to significant health benefits. For instance, choose to walk or cycle to work instead of driving, or opt for healthy snacks instead of processed foods.

Community and Support: Surround yourself with a community that supports healthy choices. Whether it is family, friends, or a fitness group, having support can motivate you to maintain your health goals.

Health is indeed your greatest wealth. By taking proactive steps to maintain and enhance your health, you ensure that you have the vitality and endurance needed to achieve your financial goals and enjoy your successes. Embrace a lifestyle that places a premium on health and watch as it transforms not only your physical state but also your financial life.

The Millennial Investor: Simple Strategies for Long-Term Wealth.

CHAPTER 24: NETWORKING AND RELATIONSHIPS: BUILDING SOCIAL CAPITAL FOR PERSONAL AND PROFESSIONAL GROWTH

Networking is much more than simply collecting contacts; it is about fostering meaningful relationships that can bring mutual benefits over time. In this chapter, we will explore the critical importance of a well-maintained network in both personal growth and career development. We will delve into effective strategies for building and nurturing these essential connections and how to leverage your network to propel your goals forward.

The Value of a Strong Network

A robust network is an invaluable asset in any professional journey. It can open doors to opportunities that might otherwise be inaccessible and provide support through knowledge, advice, and influential endorsements.

Access to Opportunities: A well-connected network can offer you job leads, partnership opportunities, or unique business ventures that are often not advertised publicly.

Knowledge and Learning: Engaging with a diverse network can expose you to valuable insights and experiences that enhance your personal and professional development.

Support and Influence: In challenging times, having a reliable network can offer both moral and strategic support to help you navigate through difficulties.
Strategies for Effective Networking

Building a successful network requires a proactive and strategic approach. It is about more than attending events; it is about forming connections that add value and meaning to both parties involved.

Engage Regularly: Make it a point to attend industry conferences, seminars, and networking events where you can meet potential contacts. Joining professional associations can also broaden your networking scope.

The Millennial Investor: Simple Strategies for Long-Term Wealth.

Utilize Social Media: Platforms like LinkedIn, Twitter, and professional groups on Facebook can be powerful tools for connecting with peers, mentors, and industry leaders. Actively update your profiles and engage with others' content to maintain visibility.

Offer Value: Always approach networking with the mindset of offering value. Whether it is sharing expertise, providing a service, or connecting people within your network, contributing positively will make others more inclined to reciprocate.

Maintaining and Nurturing Your Network
A network is only as good as how well it is maintained. Staying connected and regularly engaging with your contacts is crucial to nurturing these relationships long-term.

Consistent Communication: Use emails, social media, and occasional face-to-face meetups to stay connected. Even a simple check-in or sharing an article of mutual interest can keep the connection alive.

Personalization: Remember vital details about your contacts, such as their interests, birthdays, or major life events. Personal touches go a long way in strengthening relationships.

Professional Support: Offer your help freely, share opportunities, and provide genuine feedback. Supporting others' successes builds a foundation of goodwill and mutual respect.

Leveraging Your Network Effectively
Having a strong network is beneficial, but knowing how to effectively leverage this network can set the stage for significant advancements in your career and personal life.

Seek Advice and Mentorship: Do not hesitate to reach out to more experienced individuals in your network for advice, especially when facing new challenges or making important decisions.

Collaborate on Projects: Look for opportunities to collaborate with your contacts on projects that benefit from your combined skills and resources. This not only strengthens relationships but can also lead to innovative outcomes.

Networking Up and Sideways: While connecting with individuals in higher positions is valuable, do not overlook the benefits of networking with peers or even those at earlier stages in their careers. Everyone has something valuable to offer.

Alex's Insights: Mastering the Art of Networking

Networking has been a cornerstone of my professional growth and personal development. When I first embarked on my career journey, I underestimated the power of a strong network. However, over time, I learned that building meaningful relationships could open doors that I never knew existed and provide support in ways that were both unexpected and invaluable.

Early Networking Challenges
In the beginning, networking felt daunting. I was stepping into rooms filled with experienced professionals, feeling like an outsider. My initial approach was passive—I would attend events but barely interact, hoping somehow that mere presence would yield opportunities. It was not long before I realized that effective networking required a proactive stance.

Learning to Network Effectively
My turning point came when I decided to change my strategy. I started by setting small, achievable goals for each event, such as having meaningful conversations with at least three people. This approach not only made networking more manageable but also more rewarding.

Using Tools: I leveraged tools like LinkedIn to connect with individuals before and after events. This pre- and post-engagement helped solidify new relationships and made face-to-face interactions more comfortable and productive.

Providing Value: I learned that networking is not just about what you can get, but also what you can offer. Whether it was sharing an insightful article, offering a helpful introduction, or providing a fresh perspective on a problem, adding value to others helped me stand out and fostered reciprocal relationships.

Networking Success Stories
One of my most significant networking successes came from a chance meeting at a conference. I met a seasoned investor who was intrigued by my passion for technology startups. We exchanged ideas and contact information, and I followed up with a thoughtful thank you note. This led to a mentorship that significantly shaped my investment strategies, directly contributing to the success stories I shared in previous chapters.

Tool Utilization: Tools like meetup.com and Eventbrite became my go-to for finding relevant networking events. The targeted approach allowed me to connect with like-minded professionals and those who could provide specific guidance and opportunities aligned with my goals.

The Impact of Effective Networking
As my network grew, so did my confidence and my career opportunities. Relationships built during networking events have led to partnerships, client referrals, and even speaking engagements. Each connection added a layer of depth to my professional life and, in many ways, to my personal development as well.

Reflecting on Growth: Looking back, I attribute a huge portion of my success to the strong network I cultivated. These relationships not only opened doors but also provided a support system through various challenges.

Networking is an art that requires patience, strategy, and genuine engagement. My experience has taught me that the more you invest in building and nurturing relationships, the more you will reap the benefits in all facets of life. For anyone looking to enhance their career and personal growth, I cannot emphasize enough the power of a well-maintained network. Embrace every opportunity to connect, provide value, and grow your network—it truly can change the trajectory of your life and career.

Building and effectively managing a network is indispensable for both personal growth and professional success. By actively engaging in the cultivation of meaningful relationships and strategically leveraging these connections, you can significantly enhance your ability to achieve your goals. Remember, the quality of your network often reflects the strength of your career and personal achievements. Investing time and effort into this aspect of your development is crucial for long-term success.

CHAPTER 25: WORK-LIFE BALANCE: MAINTAINING BALANCE FOR LONG-TERM HAPPINESS AND PRODUCTIVITY

In the quest for success and achievement, it is crucial not to lose sight of the importance of a balanced life. In this chapter, we will delve into why achieving a work-life balance is essential for your overall well-being and effectiveness. We will explore familiar challenges to maintaining this balance and offer practical advice for integrating work with personal life to foster both happiness and productivity.

The Significance of Work-Life Balance

Work-life balance is not just a buzzword—it is a vital component of a healthy, productive life. Balancing professional demands with personal and family life can enhance mental health, improve relationships, and increase job satisfaction.

Here, we examine how a well-maintained balance benefits all areas of life:

Mental and Physical Health: Excessive work stress can lead to burnout, anxiety, and physical health issues. A good balance helps maintain mental clarity and physical health, enabling you to perform at your best both at work and at home.
Relationships: Spending quality time with family and friends strengthens bonds, providing emotional support that is crucial during stressful periods.

Productivity and Satisfaction: Employees who manage to balance their work and personal lives tend not only to perform better but also to experience a higher level of job satisfaction and loyalty.

Overcoming Common Challenges

Maintaining work-life balance can be particularly challenging in today's fast-paced, always-connected world. We address several obstacles and provide strategies to overcome them:

The Millennial Investor: Simple Strategies for Long-Term Wealth.

Technological Connectivity: The constant connectivity offered by smartphones and laptops can blur the lines between work and personal life. Establishing specific times when you are "off the clock" can help maintain this boundary.

High Work Demands: In careers where long hours are the norm, it can be difficult to carve out personal time. Learning to say no and delegating tasks effectively can help manage these demands.

Personal Expectations: Often, the pressure to succeed professionally pushes individuals to prioritize work over personal life. Setting realistic goals and acknowledging the importance of downtime can help recalibrate these expectations.

Strategies for Enhancing Work-Life Balance
Implementing effective strategies can help you achieve and maintain a healthy work-life balance. Here are some practical steps:

Set Clear Boundaries: Establish and communicate clear boundaries between work and personal life. This might include setting specific work hours and sticking to them, even when working from home.

Time Management Skills: Effective time management is key. Prioritize tasks, focus on being productive rather than busy, and use tools like calendars and to-do lists to keep track of both professional and personal commitments.

Use of Leave and Vacations: Make full use of your vacation time and other leave entitlements to recharge and disconnect from work pressures.

Alex's Personal Journey

From my own experience, achieving work-life balance has been a continuous journey of self-discovery and adjustment. Early in my career, I faced burnout due to my failure to balance my professional ambitions with my personal life. This experience taught me the importance of setting boundaries and taking time to recharge. Now, I make it a priority to disconnect after work hours and on weekends, which has significantly improved both my productivity at work and my personal happiness.

Work-life balance is crucial for sustainable success. By setting boundaries, managing your time effectively, and making conscious choices about how you prioritize your responsibilities, you can achieve a balance that promotes long-term happiness and productivity. Remember, a well-balanced life leads to a fulfilled life, both personally and professionally.

The Millennial Investor: Simple Strategies for Long-Term Wealth.

CONCLUSION

Conclusion: Empowering Your Financial Future

As we draw to the close of "The Millennial Investor," it's important to reflect on the journey we've undertaken together. From understanding the basics of personal finance to diving deep into investment strategies, the road to financial literacy is both challenging and rewarding.

This book has armed you with the tools to make informed decisions about your money. We started by laying a solid foundation—understanding your finances and the importance of budgeting, emergency funds, and effective debt management. Then, we explored various investment vehicles, from stocks and bonds to real estate and cryptocurrencies, offering you a broad perspective on growing your wealth.

Investing in yourself was a recurring theme, emphasizing the importance of continuous learning, maintaining good health, and nurturing relationships. These personal investments are just as crucial as financial ones, as they contribute to sustainable success and overall well-being.

The strategies discussed are not just theoretical but are drawn from real-life experiences and practical advice that can be applied regardless of your financial situation. The goal was to demystify the financial challenges and opportunities millennials face today, providing a roadmap to navigate through them with confidence.

As you move forward, remember that your financial journey is unique. What works for one person might not work for another. The key is to stay informed, be adaptable, and make decisions that align with your personal goals and values. Financial independence isn't achieved overnight, and it isn't a linear process. There will be setbacks and victories, but each step brings you closer to achieving your long-term goals.

Stay curious, remain vigilant, and continue to invest in your financial education. Your journey doesn't end here; it evolves as you grow and as the financial landscape changes. "The Millennial Investor" is your companion in this ongoing journey, helping you to navigate the complexities of personal finance with knowledge and purpose.

The Millennial Investor: Simple Strategies for Long-Term Wealth.

Thank you for joining me on this path to financial empowerment. Here's to your success, as you take control of your financial future and turn your dreams into reality. Remember, the best investment you can make is in yourself—start today, and reap the benefits for years to come. Make Sure to check the resources below for useful companies mentioned in the book.

Resources

1. **Emma** - A budgeting app that categorizes spending and helps with financial tracking.
   - Website: https://emma-app.com
2. **Monzo** - A digital bank that offers budgeting tools and instant spending notifications.
   - Website: https://monzo.com
3. **SeedInvest** - A platform that provides investment opportunities in new startups.
   - Website: https://www.seedinvest.com
4. **Kickstarter** - A crowdfunding platform to fund creative projects.
   - Website: https://www.kickstarter.com
5. **Teespring** (now known as Spring) - A platform for creating and selling custom merchandise.
   - Website: https://www.spring.com
6. **Printful** - An on-demand service that prints and ships custom designs.
   - Website: https://www.printful.com
7. **Redbubble** - A global online marketplace for print-on-demand products based on user-submitted artwork.
   - Website: https://www.redbubble.com
8. **Shopify** - An e-commerce platform for online store and retail point-of-sale systems.
   - Website: https://www.shopify.com
9. **Gumroad** - A platform that enables creators to sell products directly to their audience.
   - Website: https://www.gumroad.com
10. **Teachable** - An online platform that allows individuals to create and sell online courses
    - Website: https://www.teachable.com
11. **Udemy** - A marketplace for learning and teaching online with courses in numerous categories.
    - Website: https://www.udemy.com
12. **Trading 212** - A fintech company that offers a free, easy to use

trading platform.
- Website: https://www.trading212.com
13. **eToro** - A social trading and investment platform known for copy trading.
    - Website: https://www.etoro.com
14. **Yahoo Finance** - A website that offers financial news, data, and commentary including stock quotes, press releases, financial reports, and original content.
    - Website: https://finance.yahoo.com

The Millennial Investor: Simple Strategies for Long-Term Wealth.

Glossary

1. Asset: Anything of value owned by an individual or a company. Assets can be financial (such as stocks or bonds) or tangible (like real estate or vehicles).

2. Bonds: Debt securities issued by corporations, municipalities, or governments that pay periodic interest and return the principal amount at maturity.

3. Budget: A plan for managing income and expenses over a specified period, helping individuals or businesses allocate their resources effectively.

4. Compound Interest: The interest calculated on the initial principal, which also includes all of the accumulated interest from previous periods on a deposit or loan.

5. Cryptocurrency: Digital or virtual currencies that use cryptography for security, operating independently of a central bank.

6. Diversification: An investment strategy that involves spreading investments across various financial vehicles, industries, and other categories to reduce risk.

7. Dividends: A portion of a company's earnings distributed to shareholders, typically on a regular basis.

8. Emergency Fund: A reserved amount of money set aside to cover unexpected expenses or financial emergencies.

9. ETFs (Exchange-Traded Funds): Investment funds traded on stock exchanges, much like stocks, that hold assets such as stocks, commodities, or bonds.

10. Inflation: The rate at which the general level of prices for goods and services rises, eroding purchasing power.

11. Interest Rate: The proportion of a loan that is charged as interest to the borrower, typically expressed as an annual percentage of the loan outstanding.

12. Investment Portfolio: A collection of assets owned by an individual or institution designed to grow in value or provide income.

13. IRA (Individual Retirement Account): A retirement savings plan that provides tax advantages for retirement savings in the United States.

14. Liquidity: The ease with which an asset can be converted into cash without affecting its market price.

15. Mutual Funds: Investment programs funded by shareholders that trade in diversified holdings and are professionally managed.

16. Net Worth: The difference between the total assets and total liabilities of an individual or a company.

17. Real Estate: Property consisting of land and the buildings on it, along with its natural resources.

18. Retirement Accounts: Financial accounts (such as IRAs and 401(k)s) that are used to save and invest for retirement with various tax advantages.

19. Risk Management: The process of identification, analysis, and acceptance or mitigation of uncertainty in investment decisions.

20. Stocks: Securities that represent ownership in a corporation and represent a claim on part of the corporation's assets and earnings.

21. Trading: The action or activity of buying and selling goods and services.

www.ingramcontent.com/pod-product-compliance
Lightning Source LLC
Chambersburg PA
CBHW071213240526
45470CB00018B/1854